# Helping a Child with Nonverbal Learning Disorder or Asperger's Disorder

## — SECOND EDITION —

A Parent's Guide

### KATHRYN STEWART, PH.D.

New Harbinger Publications, Inc.

## Publisher's Note

*Care has been taken to confirm the accuracy of the information presented and to describe generally accepted practices. However, the author, editors, and publisher are not responsible for errors or omissions or for any consequences from application of the information in this book and make no warranty, express or implied, with respect to the contents of the publication.*

Distributed in Canada by Raincoast Books

Copyright © 2007 by Kathryn Stewart
New Harbinger Publications, Inc.
5674 Shattuck Avenue
Oakland, CA 94609
www.newharbinger.com

FSC
www.fsc.org
MIX
Paper from
responsible sources
FSC® C011935

Acquired by Catharine Sutker; Cover design by Amy Shoup; Edited by Jasmine Star; Text design by Tracy Carlson

Library of Congress Cataloging-in-Publication Data

Stewart, Kathryn.

Helping a child with nonverbal learning disorder or Asperger's disorder : a parent's guide / Kathryn Stewart.-- 2nd ed.

p. cm.

Rev. ed. of: Helping a child with nonverbal learning disorder or Asperger's syndrome, 2002.

Includes bibliographical references.

ISBN-13: 978-1-57224-526-6

ISBN-10: 1-57224-526-3

1. Asperger's syndrome in children. 2. Nonverbal learning disabilities. I. Stewart, Kathryn Helping a child with nonverbal learning disorder or Asperger's syndrome. II. Title.

RJ506.A9S74 2007

618.92'85889--dc22

2007023353

17   16   15

15  14  13  12  11  10  9  8  7

# Contents

# PART III
## What Now? Interventions and Program Planning

# Preface

In this second edition of *Helping a Child with Nonverbal Learning Disorder or Asperger's Disorder,* I hope to continue to provide a straight-forward, positive source of information that combines the work of other knowledgeable professionals and what I have learned over twenty years of day-to-day experience with this population of kids. Since the publication of the first edition in 2002, I have received literally thousands of e-mails from parents, kids, and professionals all over the world. The positive feedback on the book and requests for help continued to remind me of the ongoing need for information and, beyond that, action.

Our knowledge about neurocognitive disorders continues to grow, but schools and the mental health profession have been slow to catch up. Of particular concern is the confusing information presented to parents regarding diagnosis and, as a result, delayed development of appropriate interventions. I wish I could say I have the answer in this edition of the book, but I don't. Instead of more clarity, the growing body of literature has provided us with ever-increasing questions and a tendency to see *all* social functioning difficulties as Asperger's related. I do know we are overdiagnosing children with organizational and social disorders as having Asperger's. But I also know that, even with overdiagnosis, many, many children across the country are not receiving appropriate or even adequate treatment.

As the founder and director of the Orion Academy, a program dedicated to secondary education of students with neurocognitive disorders, I have found the past seven years to be an amazing experience.

Although it hasn't always been easy, those experiences have provided valuable data on what is and is not successful with our students. The students at Orion, along with their dedicated parents, have been the source of our ever-growing knowledge base. To say that I have become an expert in neurocognitive disorders is not really the truth, since it implies some finality of learning. As always, my students are my teachers, and I remain the student.

I hope this book offers you some new ideas and provides a sense that a positive future is possible for these kids. The journey we are on promises exciting developments that will help these children achieve their full potential.

# PART I

# An Overview of Nonverbal Learning Disorder and Asperger's Disorder

# 1

# What Are Nonverbal Learning Disorder and Asperger's Disorder?

For most of us, having children allows us to imagine afresh all the possibilities the world has to offer. We wish wonderful things for our children. We arrange our lives and make plans to help them succeed, we dream for them, and, in some cases, we fear for them. But no one who anxiously awaits the arrival of a new family member can imagine the pain, confusion, and turmoil that fill the life of a child with nonverbal learning disorder (NLD) or Asperger's disorder (AD). These disorders affect social communication, information processing, and organizational thinking, yet they are practically invisible.

Knowledge about and understanding of neurocognitive disorders in children is a new and expanding field. Much of what we know is from recent research and the experiences of people who struggle day to day to improve the lives of these children. The child with NLD or AD is an untapped treasure; our work is to learn the code that unlocks that treasure. This book will try to help you lessen your child's pain and confusion, not to mention your own, by offering information and practical ideas.

## ◼ Oliver's Story

*As an infant, Oliver was warm and cuddly. While awake, he spent much of his time happily playing with toys that were within reach, and he readily sought adults for closeness. He appeared precociously bright and eager to interact, often babbling in response to the vocalizations of others. Sometimes he reacted to loud noises in a frightened or pained manner, and he seemed less interested in bright visual materials than many young children are. As an older infant and a toddler, he often pointed to objects in his world and seemed to delight in the verbal responses of adults who identified the objects. He seemed less interested in exploring his world physically (his crawling and walking were slow to develop), but he was clearly interested in what went on around him. His parents were proud of his obvious intellect and they encouraged his exploration of language.*

*By age three, Oliver had developed quite an extensive vocabulary, although his motor skill development lagged behind that of other children his age. He often complained, using his excellent vocabulary, about the feel of certain articles of clothing: he wanted no tags in his clothes and preferred the feel of only certain fabrics against his skin. Although usually happy and pleasant around his parents, he could fall apart in a panic at times. He would have meltdowns, crying and screaming at a change of routine, the loss of a treasured object, or the failure of his parents to provide the correct clothing. During these meltdowns, he sometimes seemed inconsolable and his parents felt helpless to correct a problem they couldn't pin down.*

*By preschool, it was clear that Oliver was unusual. Although warm and loving at home and generally well behaved, he had few friends at school and rarely engaged in cooperative play. He desired contact with his age-mates but was clumsy in activities requiring motor skills and had real trouble understanding how to engage a peer in a mutual activity. Other children would ignore him, and he was often found playing alone. At home he established a routine that his parents learned well. He developed specific habits that he adhered to. He also developed a special interest in dinosaurs: he knew the scientific names of the different dinosaurs and could correctly identify the time periods in which they lived. It annoyed him, even at age five, that movies incorrectly portrayed dinosaurs from different periods as coexisting.*

## What Is a Neurocognitive Disorder?

Neurocognitive disorders (also known as neurobehavioral disorders) are dysfunctions in the brain's processing of information. Such a dysfunction is a learning disability or a developmental disorder and it can be inherited. Sometimes it is inherent to the child, or it can be the result of a brain trauma (seizure or brain injury, for example). It is not a retardation of any type, but a difference in processing information, all kinds of information, that creates difficulties in understanding the world and interacting with others. The disorder may impact learning, social functioning, and motor activities. It may be mild or severe, and some areas may be more affected than others and may continue to impact the child throughout her life in some form.

There are many types of neurocognitive or neurobehavioral disorders; nonverbal learning disorder and Asperger's disorder are but two. Although they are separate diagnoses, these two disorders have some striking similarities in their symptoms, and because there is a definite overlap of successful interventions, it is reasonable to cover them in the same book.

## Learning Disabilities in General

The concept of learning disabilities has been around since educators became interested in understanding why apparently bright kids could not perform well in school. A learning disability is an inability to learn material and to perform or produce work at a level equal to one's potential or intelligence. If a child has a potential well below average or an IQ measured in the low-average range or below, a learning disability would not be involved when that child's performance is below average. In that case, the child would be performing and learning at her potential and would not have a learning disability. Children with learning disabilities are by definition bright children—an important point to make to them when helping them understand their learning needs.

In the 1970s and on into the 1980s, educators, clinicians, and researchers began to focus on language-based learning disabilities. They identified children who were primarily failing in reading or, in some cases, failing in both reading and math. Over time, there was a growing understanding of specific learning disabilities, among them dyslexia. These children became the focus of a concerted effort by researchers, educators, and parents that resulted in the development of many successful programs aimed at remediating these specific learning disabilities. That was almost twenty years ago, and now dyslexia is a well-understood learning disorder with a good prognosis. Today, we find ourselves on the threshold of that same kind of explosion of information and program development for children with NLD or AD. Since 2000, programs like the Orion Academy in California and an increasing body of research into these disorders across the world have contributed to expanded information on diagnosis, causes, and treatment. Social dysfunction and organizational deficits are now seen as specific areas of need in these learning disabilities, requiring specific educational interventions.

# Nonverbal Learning Disorder

Beginning in the late 1960s, researchers began to notice children with specific deficits in social-emotional functioning and poor math skills (Johnson and Myklebust 1971). These children were unlike those with traditional learning disabilities in that they did not seem to suffer language-based difficulties, yet they exhibited a consistent cluster of problems all their own. Such children could generally be described as socially inept, physically clumsy, and having difficulty with math and general visual-spatial processing but able to generate language extremely well. From these observations, the first description was published of what would become known as nonverbal learning disorder (Myklebust 1975).

Interest in these children continued, and in 1989, the first book devoted to NLD was published: *Nonverbal Learning Disabilities: The Syndrome and the Model*, by Byron Rourke. In this book, Rourke describes these children as having difficulties in five major areas:

1. Tactile perception. The understanding of how things feel includes knowing an object by feel (silk is smooth and pavement rough) but also being able to ignore the feel of certain things (the tag in the back of a shirt, for instance).

2. Psychomotor coordination. This is the ability to direct actions in a coordinated manner—for example, throwing a baseball while running.

3. Visual-spatial organization. This involves using information received from the sense of sight to know things about the environment. Examples include understanding that things that are closer appear larger and those that are farther away appear smaller, or looking at a page full of math problems and knowing where one ends and another begins. Visual-spatial organization also controls the ability to maneuver around objects in one's path when walking or running.

4. Nonverbal problem solving. This skill involves knowing how something goes together without having a manual to describe it. Nonverbal problem solving is likely to involve visual-spatial skills, so it makes sense that if performance is poor in one area it would be poor in the other as well.

5. Ability to appreciate incongruities and humor. Ability to appreciate incongruities, or things that don't go together, and an appreciation for humor seem to be related skills.

The children with NLD studied by Rourke (1989) had significant difficulties understanding either incongruities or the humor of other people. However, they had well-developed rote verbal skills (accurate, specific use of words), verbal memory skills, and auditory linguistic skills (the ability to remember information they heard). They memorized information or facts very well, a process called rote learning, especially information presented to them verbally. They could easily memorize and repeat back math facts, spelling words, or a list of baseball statistics. These children seemed to remember things they heard, often exceptionally well.

The early researchers speculated that these children suffered from a dysfunction of the right hemisphere of the brain (see figure 1.1), which was considered to be the source of imaginative thinking, visual-spatial processing, and ideas and thinking that rely on nonverbal understanding of the world. Individuals who demonstrate strong right-hemisphere skills can easily see how something should fit together, not needing verbal or written instructions. In the past, mathematics was considered a right-brain activity, as was the ability to read nonverbal social cues, including body language, facial expression, and even tone of voice.

Traditionally, language skills were seen as the domain of the left hemisphere of the brain. But researchers believed that without help or

Figure 1.1    View of the Brain from Above

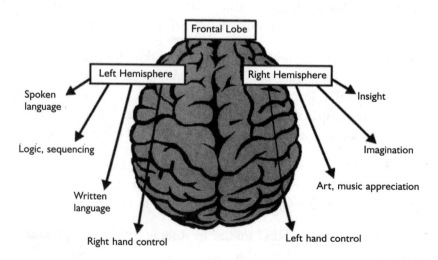

instruction from the right hemisphere, language skills did not include social skills. It was thought that a disorder of the right brain would interfere with the person's ability to read social situations. Such a person could produce a large volume of language without understanding the social nuances of that language.

## The Brain: Current Understanding

Early views held that the brain developed by age five and that from then on nothing new occurred, but we know now that brain functioning is more plastic (or changeable) and resilient than had been thought. Understanding the functioning of the brain as skill sets divided into right and left hemispheres is far too simplistic a view. The brain has layers of connections, from deep within the interior of the brain to the folds on the surface, all serving a purpose. Scientists have begun to map the complex and overlapping functions of different parts of the brain, and one finding is that various types of learning and thinking appear not to be limited to one hemisphere. Instead, the many aspects of learning cross between the two hemispheres and involve other brain areas.

The central role of the frontal lobe (see figure 1.1) has become clearer. Among its many jobs, the frontal lobe is responsible for developing and then supervising the connections between pieces of information stored elsewhere in the brain. One very important job of the frontal lobe seems to be enabling us to learn from new information; in other words, it allows us to use novel situations to increase knowledge. Information from both the right and left hemispheres connects with the frontal lobe, and through complex and poorly understood brain actions, learning occurs. The ability to integrate information from different events, times, or sources of information, which is key to success in the world as an adult, is one of the higher cognitive functions that are part of the executive function of the brain. Understanding these executive functioning skills is emerging as an important aspect of addressing deficits in AD and NLD.

## NLD and the Brain

Currently, NLD is understood as going beyond a failure of functioning of the right hemisphere. The problems experienced by children with NLD in reading social situations, integrating novel information, and learning from experiences suggest a dysfunction of the frontal lobe and the white matter—the neural connections between the right and left hemispheres of the brain and the frontal lobe. The term "nonverbal learning disorder" is actually misleading and unfortunate, as the difficulties experienced are not simply nonverbal, and their scope goes far beyond the problems involved in a learning disability. As you will see in later chapters, children with NLD are not without problems in language. Their problems are not in language production, but in language use. Some professionals working with people with NLD have suggested that a more appropriate name for the disorder would be information processing disorder (IPD, if we stick to the shorthand used for other diagnoses). But for now, nonverbal learning disorder (or nonverbal learning disability) is the agreed-upon term applied to the children described here.

## Asperger's Disorder and the Brain

Brain research in regard to Asperger's disorder has generated more information than we currently have for NLD. However, issues around inconsistent research conditions, specifically what criteria are used for a diagnosis of AD, complicate much of the research. But a growing body of information suggests that the processing of information by individuals with AD differs from that of neurotypical (NT) individuals, that is, people without a neurocognitive disorder. As an example, research using neuroimaging with Asperger's patients suggests a possible interplay between lesions in the areas of the brain connecting the temporal and occipital lobes and deficits in perception of facial expression and eye gaze (Puce et al. 1998; Schultz et al. 1997). The ability to accurately interpret facial expression and maintain eye contact are important skills for social success, and without them, a child is at a definite disadvantage. This type of research is important in developing better diagnosis and allowing for early intervention.

## How Common Is NLD?

In an annual report to Congress in 1999, the U.S. Department of Education (1999) stated that 12.8 percent of all children enrolled in school in the United States were in special education. Over 8 percent of U.S. schoolchildren are specifically qualified for special education in areas of learning disabilities and speech and language impairment, both of which often afflict children with NLD. Byron Rourke reports that 10 percent of the children in populations with learning disorders do, in fact, have NLD (Rourke 1995). This suggests that approximately 1 percent of the general U.S. population, or approximately 2.7 million people, currently have NLD. There seems to be no difference in incidence between girls and boys. Because diagnosis of NLD is not consistent and because NLD isn't recognized by school districts as a specific learning disability, there is reason to believe that these numbers are a gross underrepresentation of true extent of the disorder.

Symptoms and diagnosis will be discussed in more detail later in this book, but the principal areas of dysfunction in nonverbal learning disorder are as follows:

- Deficits in information processing and organizational skills

- Poor visual-spatial functioning and sensory integration ability

- Deficits in working memory

- Slow processing speed

- Significant impairment of social interactions

At the same time, children with NLD generally excel in the following areas:

- Verbal language production (beyond age level)

- Vocabulary

- Retention of factual information

- Learning and remembering information that has been heard

## Diagnosis of Nonverbal Learning Disorder

Nonverbal learning disorder is not formally recognized in the most recent edition of the *Diagnostic and Statistical Manual of Mental Disorders (DSM-IV)*, the official guide to diagnosing mental disorders published by the American Psychiatric Association (APA 1994). However, a diagnosis of NLD can usually be made by a competent psychologist or behavioral pediatrician using a variety of diagnostic tools, including taking a history, performing an interview, and referring the child for testing and other evaluations. A competent assessment will include a written report that addresses the areas of strengths and deficits found. Specific recommendations addressing both strengths and deficits should be included. Here are some details on what should be included in the evaluation:

1. **Interview of the child and the parents.** A clinical psychologist, psychiatrist, or behavioral pediatrician conducts this interview, which reviews history and current functioning.

2. **Formal assessment by a psychologist or neuropsychologist.** Be sure the person is licensed and has experience both with the tests listed below and with evaluating children for NLD and AD. The following tests are recommended:

   - Wechsler Intelligence Scale for Children-IV (WISC-IV). The newest version of the Wechsler tests, this is a test of overall intelligence for children ages six to sixteen. This version has fifteen subtests that assess four areas: verbal comprehension, perceptual reasoning, working memory, and processing speed. The specific scores on these subtests are more relevant to diagnosis than the overall IQ scores. The subtest scores range from 2 to 19, with an average of 10. The four areas assessed are used to determine four IQ indexes, one in each area, along with an overall IQ score—the full-scale IQ. An IQ between 90 and 110 is considered average. For most average children, there won't be more than a 12-point difference between indexes, but children with NLD often show a huge difference between these scores, with verbal comprehension scores exceeding perceptual reasoning scores by 20 or more points. Given that the WISC-IV is a newer version of the WISC and has new indexes, research has not been done on score differences between the four indexes. But the subtest scores of particular interest for diagnosis of NLD (Rourke 1998) remain the same; we expect lowered scores for tasks involving visual-spatial organization (object assembly, block design, and coding) and higher scores for tasks involving auditory perception, language skills, and general understanding of language (comprehension, vocabulary, and similarities). We also expect to see lowered processing-speed scores relative to verbal comprehension. Working memory scores hold potential for future research, as this is an area of deficit for many children with NLD.

■ Kaufman Assessment Battery for Children (K-ABC). This test, for children ages five to eleven, gives valuable information to compare to the WISC-III and offers information on learning style and nonverbal functioning. It is not often offered, but it is an excellent tool in the overall assessment.

- Vineland Adaptive Behavior Scale (VABS). This test assesses personal and social functioning through an interview with a parent or caregiver.

- Personality Inventory for Children (PIC). This inventory, which assesses behavior, emotions, and cognitive status, is completed by a parent or another adult who knows the child well.

- Rey-Osterrieth Complex Figure Test (ROCF). This test analyzes various aspects of visual-spatial ability and memory in people of all ages.

- Category Test. Various forms of category tests measure concept learning and examine flexibility of thinking and openness to learning.

- Sentence Memory Test. These tests assess memory of meaningful units of language.

- Trail Making Test (TMT; forms A and B). These tests assess visual scanning, visual-motor speed, and visual-spatial ability.

- Specific subtests from neuropsychological assessment tools such as the Halstead-Reitan Neurological Test Battery (HRNTB). These might include tactile form recognition, grooved pegboard, fingertip number writing, grip strength, and target test.

3. **Educational assessment.** This is usually done by the school district. If your district is not qualified to assess the child's educational level adequately, seek out an educational therapist or educational psychologist. Either the WIAT or the Woodcock-Johnson is needed, along with all the others listed. Additional tests are often included, especially if the assessment indicates that any areas merit further inquiry.

- Wechsler Individual Achievement Test (WIAT). This test assesses arithmetic, listening comprehension, oral expression, reading, spelling, and writing skills.

- Woodcock-Johnson Test III. This two-part test, which measures general intellectual ability, specific cognitive abilities, scholastic aptitude, oral language, and academic achievement, is useful for identifying children with average or above-average intelligence who suffer from learning disabilities.

- Wide Range Achievement Test (WRAT). This measure of reading recognition, spelling, and arithmetic computation can be helpful for identifying learning disabilities and developing programs to address them.

- Test of Written Language (TOWL). This test identifies low achievement, strengths and weaknesses, and can be used to document the child's progress over time.

- Writing sample—both sentences and paragraphs. The sample is evaluated for written-language level.

4. **Occupational therapy assessment.** A qualified occupational therapist must make this assessment, which should evaluate sensory integration and perceptual abilities, balance, and motor skills. Specific recommendations for school and home are needed and should include posture exercises and recommendations for the most appropriate desks and chairs.

5. **Speech therapy evaluation.** A qualified speech and language specialist must make this assessment. The focus of the evaluation should be on pragmatic language, and it should include tests such as the Comprehensive Assessment of Spoken Language (CASL), Test of Pragmatic Language (TOPL), and a language sample in different settings, including child to adult and child to peer. Evaluation of language samples by a speech and language therapist can be a very

valuable tool. Use of a pragmatic language checklist of some sort (similar to the one included in chapter 2 of this book) is an important measure of the child's functioning level.

6. **Nonverbal and social skills level.** A psychologist experienced in social skills training can evaluate the functional level of the child's social skills. The Diagnostic Analysis of Nonverbal Accuracy (DANVA) can evaluate the ability to read and to send nonverbal messages. It is relatively new, and there are a limited number of clinicians who are familiar with it, but it may prove valuable in an overall assessment.

As you can see, the diagnostic criteria are fairly technical. If your child hasn't been diagnosed and you're wondering whether NLD is a possibility, you can use the questionnaire below to help you decide whether a professional assessment is in order. This symptom list, which I developed together with Dr. Darlene Sweetland in 2001 for screening for NLD, was updated in 2006 and revised for a general audience.

## NLD SYMPTOM LIST

If a child's characteristics have an 80 percent or greater agreement with the items in the following list, there's a high likelihood of NLD and a professional assessment is in order. Check off all items that apply to the child. If you check off twenty-two or more items, seek a competent professional assessment.

### Social and Emotional Indicators

_____ 1. Poor ability to read the facial and behavioral cues of others, especially peers.

_____ 2. Concrete or literal interpretation of language in social situations; missing the social nuances.

_____ 3. Excessive concern with fairness.

_____ 4. Very black-and-white interpretation of rules: The child considers rules important in dealing with peers, adults, and learning situations and will become upset when a rule is broken.

_____ 5. Inconsolableness: Once upset, the child finds it difficult to let go of the upset.

_____ 6. Rigid thinking: Once the child has formed an idea about something, he or she does not want to deviate from that idea.

_____ 7. Diagnosis of an anxiety disorder made by a psychologist or psychiatrist (this disorder may be mild to severe).

_____ 8. Being prone to frustration: The child often has triggers or circumstances that feel especially frustrating. These can include hearing certain sounds, sensing pressure to react or interact, or feeling confused about what is being asked of him or her.

_____ 9. Sudden outbursts: These are usually intermittent but have predictable triggers; outbursts can involve verbalization, physical activity directed at objects, or tantrums.

_____ 10. Poor grooming and hygiene: The child or teen appears to have no sense of personal presentation, nor of the impact he or she has on others.

_____ 11. Sleep difficulties, either current or in the past.

## Language Use

_____ 12. No history of language delays: In early development, the child's language developed normally or better than normal.

_____ 13. High output of language: The child can sound like a "little professor."

_____ 14. Distorted prosody (the rhythm and flow of speech): Many children with NLD speak in a monotone.

_____ 15. Excellent verbal production (a large vocabulary) in a child who performs below expectations academically.

_____ 16. Problems with pragmatic language (understanding and using language correctly in context, which involves understanding the intent of the language) in a child with excellent verbal production: This means children with NLD may not use language as well as they can produce it.

_____ 17. Development of expertise in topics of interest, often in a manner that is overly focused on those topics: A child with NLD will want to talk at great length about the topic, unaware of the disinterest of his or her audience. Topics may change over time.

## Cognitive or Learning Indicators

_____ 18. Inability to pretend: This does not mean the child does not engage in fantasy thinking; however, this fantasy thinking is often related to a preoccupation with a movie, TV series, video game, or book.

_____ 19. Disorganization: Although they can be highly perfectionistic, children with NLD often cannot organize their thinking, their work, or their routines. They tend to lose assignments, papers, notes, and so on.

_____ 20. Difficulty with time (learning to tell time or understanding the meaning of time segments): For example, the child can read the clock, especially digital clocks and tell you what time it is but really does not seem to have a conceptual understanding of time. At 9:45, the child can tell you that there are fifteen minutes until 10:00, but he or she has no real sense of how long fifteen minutes is.

_____ 21. Confusion determining right from left: This is often described as directional confusion.

_____ 22. Deficits in nonrote learning: The child will do better at memorizing facts (rote learning) than at inferring meaning or predicting outcomes. The child will have trouble with questions along the lines of "What would happen next?"

_____ 23. Good decoding skills: Reading scores will be average or above.

_____ 24. Poor or lowered comprehension scores: Understanding the main idea is particularly difficult.

_____ 25. Dependence on auditory information as support for other learning tasks: The child will often self-talk through difficult activities at home or school or in public.

## Sensory-Motor Indicators

_____ 26. Tactile sensitivity: The child reports that things "feel funny" or has preferences for clothing or blankets with a certain feel. When younger, the child may have wanted all tags cut out of his or her clothes.

_____ 27. Auditory sensitivity: Sounds bother the child, and he or she has difficulty screening out extra noises. Children with NLD often report that people chewing gum or tapping pencils in a classroom or public setting is distracting to them.

_____ 28. Tendency to get "lost in space": The child is easily disoriented, actually becoming lost in places he or she has been before. This tendency will be heightened in new or highly stressful situations.

_____ 29. Motor skill problems that usually manifest as one or more of the following:

- Dysgraphia (impaired ability to produce written words or symbols as a result of a brain dysfunction)

- Gross motor difficulties, for example, problems riding a bike or playing sports or a tendency to bump into things

- Lack of stamina; easily tired by sports

- Fine motor problems in skills other than writing, for example, learning to tie shoelaces

## Asperger's Disorder

Asperger's disorder has been a recognized, if somewhat ignored, diagnosis since it was first described by Hans Asperger in 1944. Awareness of the disorder increased in the United States following publication of a clinical account of the syndrome by Lorna Wing in 1981. Yet it wasn't until Asperger's and its diagnostic criteria appeared in the *DSM-IV* (APA 1994) as a childhood developmental disorder in the area of pervasive developmental disorders that the disorder began to be studied, discussed, and reviewed with discerning interest. This interest has been partially sparked by the desire to develop an understanding of the overlap between Asperger's disorder, high-functioning autism, and NLD. Given the inconsistencies in diagnosis of AD and the fact that Asperger's disorder is often included in autism data and considered part of autism spectrum disorders, it is difficult to know the exact numbers.

According to a study in fourteen states conducted by the Autism Developmental Disorders Monitoring Network (2007), autism spectrum disorders may occur in as many as one in every 150 eight-year-old-children in the United States. It is important to note that

Asperger's disorder is included in these numbers; however, the actual number of children with Asperger's disorder, specifically, is unclear. The National Institute of Neurological Disorders and Stroke (2007) has put forth statistics suggesting that Asperger's disorder may occur in one in five thousand children in the United States. The fact that Asperger's disorder is more common than Hans Asperger originally suggested is clear. Yet accurate statistics will remain elusive until consistency in diagnosis is achieved.

## ■ Wren's Story

*As an infant, Wren seemed to enjoy being held but she cried often and had feeding problems. She was her parent's first child, and they were not concerned that her speech, although developing normally, was focused on certain things. Specifically, Wren had a small, pink toy pony made of silky fabric that she had to have with her. She rubbed it on her face and smelled it often. She talked about the pink pony and the many horse and pony miniatures she had collected. At age five, she still kept the pink pony with her at all times, even bringing it to school. Her language was developing well; she had a large vocabulary that her parents were proud of. Yet she did not play with other children and did not want anyone except her mother or father to touch her. She was clumsy and couldn't ride a bike or tie her shoes, but she could do almost any puzzle given to her. Her food choices became more limited and she preferred to have the same thing every day—macaroni and cheese and milk. She often woke during the night, although she denied having bad dreams. Her parents were not concerned; they saw her as shy and imagined that she would grow up to be someone who did not like groups. Her mother and father, both professionals with computer technology careers, had both been shy growing up, and they saw no problem with their daughter's shyness.*

## Common Characteristics of Asperger's Disorder

Children with NLD or Asperger's are characterized by normal or accelerated language development but poor social, or pragmatic, language. Unlike children with autism and even high-functioning autism, these children have a desire to form relationships that goes beyond getting needs met by other people; yet they often fail in their attempts to socialize. Children with AD show a greater degree of social ineptitude than children with NLD. They are also particularly likely to have special interests in which they achieve "expert status." These areas of special interest often develop into obsessions, and the rigidity of the child's thinking in these areas can be a source of much difficulty. This rigid thinking can occur in many areas of their lives and take others by surprise, as these children can appear most reasonable and quite bright, leading others to assume they will react as a typical child or person would.

Here's an example: In a pre-algebra class, a very bright ninth-grader at the Orion Academy was asked to complete a task of finding grocery ads in a newspaper and putting them into a large book that would later be used as a basis of mathematical calculations. The task was described as "making your own grocery store." The teacher felt this activity, which wasn't really the math activity, just a lead-in, would be very easy and hopefully fun. This particular student sat through the period choosing a number of food items but not putting them into his book. The teacher made numerous attempts to get him started, trying to help him get his "grocery store" completed. By the end of day two, when the other students had moved on to doing math calculations, he was still stuck and becoming increasingly agitated. Finally, in response to the teacher's frustrated inquiry why he wouldn't just glue those ads into his grocery store, he burst out with "It's not a grocery store. It's a catalogue." Realizing the problem had been one of language translation and the student's rigid thinking, the teacher quickly said, "Of course it's a catalogue; please complete it," and he did in short order.

Like children with NLD, children with Asperger's also have excellent vocabularies, even while they fail at the pragmatic or day-to-day use of language. Yet, unlike children with NLD, there appears to be a subgroup with the AD diagnosis that may do well at certain tasks involving visual detail (drawing or seeing a detail that is missing in a drawing or on an object) and certain visual motor tasks (doing puzzles or mazes or copying things). The inability to produce written work is a central theme in both disorders. In Asperger's, as opposed to NLD, this difficulty may not involve dysgraphia (problems with the act of writing). Rather, it is a result of a breakdown in the child's ability to turn thoughts into written work. This is a processing problem at the level of brain functioning rather than a motor problem with physically producing letters and words.

## Diagnosing Asperger's Disorder

The currently accepted criteria for diagnosing Asperger's disorder are from the *DSM-IV* (APA 1994). Having an agreed-upon set of criteria for diagnosis allows professionals to maintain a clear and concise dialogue. Without established criteria, it is impossible to know if one doctor's idea of AD is the same as another's.

The major areas for diagnosis of AD are as follows (APA 1994):

1.  Qualitative impairment in social interaction, which includes at least two of the following areas:

    ■ Serious difficulty with nonverbal behaviors, such as eye contact or reading and understanding facial expression, body postures, and social gestures

    ■ Problems making friends

    ■ No spontaneous desire to share enjoyment, interests, or achievements with others

    ■ Lack of social or emotional reciprocity

2.  Restricted, repetitive, and stereotyped patterns of behavior, interest, and activities, with at least one of the following:

- Encompassing preoccupation with one or more restricted interests that is abnormal in either intensity or focus

- Apparently inflexible adherence to specific, nonfunctional routines or rituals

- Stereotyped and repetitive motor mannerisms (such as hand or finger flapping or twisting or complex whole-body movements)

- A preoccupation with parts of things or objects

3. The disturbance causes clinically significant impairment in social, occupational, or other important areas of functioning.

4. There is no clinically significant general delay in language (for example, single words used by age two and communicative phrases used by age three).

5. There is no clinically significant delay in cognitive development or in the development of age-appropriate self-help skills, adaptive behavior (other than in social interaction), and curiosity about the environment in childhood.

6. Criteria are not met for another specific pervasive developmental disorder or schizophrenia.

# Asperger's, NLD, and High-Functioning Autism

Although Asperger's disorder, unlike NLD, has diagnostic criteria defined in *DSM-IV* (APA 1994), it remains an area of debate whether Asperger's is a subgroup of autism (similar to high-functioning autism, as some authors contend) or a separate developmental disorder with separate neurological issues. This uncertainty underlies one of the major roadblocks to useful discussion about AD in the professional community, as various programs for and research on people with

AD may be addressing different groups of individuals with different issues. This confusion creates difficulty in using the research data in any meaningful manner.

However, the work of Fred Volkmar, MD, and Ami Klin, MD, at the Yale Child Study Center is an excellent source of information on Asperger's, and their research into diagnostic indicators and specific issues such as facial recognition and social development offer hope for the future. In their article "Asperger Disorder," they state, "Several lines of evidence suggest important differences among Asperger's disorder, autism, and pervasive developmental disorder not otherwise specified. In a *DSM-IV* field trial, for example, patients with a clinical diagnosis of Asperger's disorder were found to differ in several ways from those with autism and those with pervasive developmental disorder not otherwise specified. The patients with Asperger's disorder had higher verbal performance IQs than those with autism and significantly greater social impairment than those with pervasive developmental disorder not otherwise specified" (Volkmar et al. 2000, 265).

Although some parents and professionals describe Asperger's as a type of high-functioning autism, the idea that Asperger's is a version of autism is highly debatable. There is, as yet, little agreement in the field, but some researchers speculate that autism and Asperger's cannot be the same thing, because autism appears to be a dysfunction of the left hemisphere (Dawson et al. 1986) and, as such, is not at all the same neurobehavioral disorder. To complicate matters, both NLD and Asperger's are disorders with a wide range of symptoms. Two children with the diagnosis of Asperger's disorder may not seem at all alike. This is hardly good news, either to parents or to the professional community. More research is needed to more clearly sort out these related disorders, and consistent use of existing diagnostic criteria is required to be sure any two professionals (or parents) are talking about the same type of disorder when they define a child as having Asperger's. Without this consistency, developing a program for the child is difficult, and parents are left to wonder which of all the suggested interventions are really right for their child.

In reviewing the existing diagnostic criteria for Asperger's and autism, the central distinctions between children with Asperger's or

NLD and children with autism, even high-functioning autism, have to do with language:

| Asperger's disorder | Nonverbal learning disorder | High-functioning autism |
|---|---|---|
| Normal language development by age three | Normal language development by age three | Language delay or unusual development by age three |
| Language used to interact | Language used to interact | Language used to get needs met |

Autism is usually diagnosed before the age of five, and the diagnosis of high-functioning autism (HFA) is likely to be considered for a child whose early diagnosis was autism and who then progresses (usually through intervention) to develop more normal-appearing language over time. HFA is usually associated with increasing language skill as the child matures and with a higher IQ than is often seen in autism. To further complicate matters, those with HFA often develop the ability to use language to interact with the world more effectively than the autistic individual. This leads clinicians and parents to assume that the child who was autistic is now, because of better language use, more appropriately diagnosed as having Asperger's. Given that these are separate diagnostic categories, the new diagnosis would not follow logically, yet it is a way of thinking that is all too common.

Research examining the characteristics of HFA, AD, and NLD found significant similarities between characteristics of Asperger's and NLD and also found that both NLD and Asperger's differ from HFA. "Regardless of whether or not AD and HFA are truly different diagnostic entities, the significant divergence of neuropsychological profiles suggests that intervention strategies for AD should be of a different nature, directly addressing specific neuropsychological deficits and building on neuropsychological assets, an approach that has been described as very useful with individuals with Nonverbal Learning Disabilities" (Klin et al. 1995, 256).

There is no simple answer to this issue, nor is there consensus at this time. As we have seen, the current classification system for disorders, the *DSM-IV*, includes Asperger's disorder as a pervasive developmental disorder, in the same category as autism, while NLD is not included at all. Yet distinguishing among these disorders is important as it impacts accurate diagnosis as well as effective treatment. Unfortunately, until we have an agreed-upon diagnostic continuum with clear guidelines, confusion about the lines between the categories will remain.

## The Overlap of NLD and Asperger's Disorder

NLD and Asperger's are definitely not the same disorder. However, it has been suggested that they are, in fact, different stops along the same line, that is, that they represent different variations of a similar dysfunction of the brain. In any case, as both disorders involve a high level of verbal skills, similar difficulties in processing information and engaging in social interaction, and a need for a specialized learning environment, I believe that children with these two disorders benefit from many of the same interventions.

All of these children display various deficiencies in social and interactive skills, and they often use language in idiosyncratic ways. They have normal-to-excellent language development, even accelerated development in some cases, but others perceive their use of language as off or odd. And although they want to form relationships, they find it hard to negotiate the complications of social interactions.

Volkmar and Klin (1998) reported a study they conducted comparing the criteria for diagnosis of NLD and Asperger's. Among other things, they reported finding six areas of deficits in both NLD and Asperger's and five areas of deficits that neither NLD nor AD children had. These areas are as follows:

## Poor Performance

1. Fine motor skills (writing, shoe tying, stringing beads)

2. Gross motor skills (bike riding, sports, running, dancing)

3. Visual-motor integration (hand-to-eye activities, such as filling in a bubble on a test sheet)

4. Visual-spatial integration (judging proximity, seeing details, being able to tell foreground from background)

5. Nonverbal concept formation ("seeing" something in your mind, using inspiration, dealing with new ideas)

6. Visual memory (remembering things you see)

## Good Performance

1. Articulation (making the sounds of speech)

2. Verbal output (talking, producing words in meaningful speech)

3. Auditory perception (understanding things one hears)

4. Vocabulary (knowledge of words and word use)

5. Verbal memory (remembering things one hears)

Although somewhat dated at this point, *Asperger's Syndrome*, by Tony Attwood (1997) is a good book on the topic that continues to provide useful basic information for both professionals and parents. Attwood's description of the strengths and weaknesses of children with Asperger's makes clear the many similarities between Asperger's and NLD. However, the two disorders are separate and the need for accurate diagnosis is central to effective intervention. Children with both of these conditions are frequently misdiagnosed with autism or attention-deficit disorder and, as a result, often don't receive appropriate treatment programs. In addition to books and journal articles, numerous websites address issues relating to AD and NLD. (See appendix A for a list of some of the websites.)

## ■ Oliver's Story (continued)

*Oliver entered kindergarten and his parents heard many characterizations of his behavior, ranging from "spoiled" (because of his tantrums and rigid insistence on things being done in a specific manner) to "severely disturbed" (because of his inability to interact socially and his unusual use of language). Parents and teachers alike offered their opinions, many suggesting that Oliver suffered from attention-deficit disorder. Oliver's parents, being conscientious people, could not ignore these well-meaning opinions, and they began to have Oliver evaluated by a series of professionals in their community. These professionals suggested stimulant medication and parenting books to help them "control" Oliver, but his parents saw no positive changes as a result of either strategy. By the end of kindergarten, Oliver had no friends, continued to use language unsuccessfully as his primary means of interaction, and had received no real intervention for his deficits in visual-spatial processing, motor skills, or social interactions. He had no idea how to "read" another person and continued with his concrete, literal interpretation of language.*

*For example, Oliver's teacher explained his frustration in dealing with Oliver with this story: "One day while sitting in a circle with the class, Oliver took a small train from his pocket and began playing with it [Oliver is an expert on trains]. I saw him and told him, "I don't want to see you playing with that again; if I do, I'll have to take it away." Oliver listened politely, then stood up and went to another area of the classroom, where he turned his back and began playing with the train. When I became angry and sent Oliver to the office for being "smart," Oliver had no idea what he had done. As he explained later, "You told me you didn't want to see me playing with that ... so I moved."*

# 2

# Areas of Strength and Weakness

For parents who are confronting the diagnosis of their child for the first time, it may seem that all the professionals can see are the "problems" their child has. Those who spend time with these youngsters—parents and professionals alike—know that indeed the deficits are significant and should not be ignored. Yet there is more to any individual than his problems, and a good assessment will address both strengths and weaknesses. As a group, children with NLD or Asperger's have predictable clusters of strengths and weaknesses. Knowing about both allows parents and professionals to more appropriately plan programs and evaluate experiences that will be successful for these children. However, each child is unique, and although the descriptions in this chapter generally hold true, each individual will be unique and may or may not have many of the weaknesses and strengths discussed here.

## The Good News First: Strengths

As a group, children with NLD or AD are bright, inquisitive learners who nevertheless often perform below expectations in traditional academic settings. The fact that, as a group, these students want to learn is a valuable strength. Unfortunately, with repeated experiences of failure, this desire to learn can disappear. As we will see in part

II, there are many interconnected reasons these children fail, ranging from specific learning disabilities to inappropriate educational settings and academic expectations. In addition—and this may be a surprise to many—at times the accommodations designed to help these students end up creating a whole series of other problems that, in the long run, reinforce their "disabled" label.

## *Rote Learning*

Some authors have described younger children with NLD or AD as excelling at rote learning and memorization of facts (Thompson 1996)—sometimes math or spelling facts or facts relating to a specific area of interest. This view is not entirely supported by ongoing work with NLD students over the past ten years. While children with NLD or AD often do seem proficient at rote learning or memorization of facts specific to an area of interest, memorizing math facts is not a consistently acquired skill and varies greatly from student to student. More often, learning math facts remains a serious difficulty for those with NLD throughout their lives, and this contributes to poor performance in math as they struggle to recall these facts and lose the concept of the entire problem.

In addition, it is important to note that learning rote information does not mean these children can call forth facts when needed in class, nor does it mean they can use the information in a meaningful manner. In fact, so-called skills in rote learning can become a weakness if teachers and parents do not specifically teach concepts in addition to facts. Reliance on facts, such as memorizing multiplication tables without understanding the concept behind multiplication, will greatly limit the child's ability to progress in math and, later, in other subjects such as science.

### ■ Michael's Story

*Michael is eleven years old, and until sixth grade, he loved to learn. He has poor social skills, or so he is told, although he isn't sure exactly what that means. He doesn't have any friends, and at lunchtime he eats alone. But he does know he can remember anything about World War II fighter planes and can honestly say he enjoys thinking about those planes, looking at pictures of them in books, and talking about them. This past year in school he began to feel that maybe he isn't as smart as his parents keep telling him he is. He can't do the reports his teacher assigns, he can't get his homework done, and he has trouble with tests, which he never can finish in time. He used to feel pretty good about school, but now there is no time for his special interest and his teacher doesn't care about it anyway.*

## Special Interests

Many children with NLD or AD take great pleasure in learning facts about a topic of interest and will describe this as relaxing. However, although it may be pleasant and relaxing, focusing on this type of activity can cause problems. Let's use as an example a child who memorizes facts about a sports team. The gathering of these facts—reading and rereading, and acquiring information from websites, magazines, trading cards, and other sources—is ongoing. The child amasses a great number of facts. Yet as the information increases, he has no internal organizational system—no hierarchy for ordering the information as more or less important. All information is of equal importance and is thus difficult to use in a meaningful way.

Furthermore, the child, although knowledgeable about the sports team and its players, never wants to attend a real sports event. The actual game, the players, and the drama and suspense of the sport are not important. Knowing facts like players' names and statistics about them never translates into an interest in the real players or the real team. In fact, it may never translate into information for a conversation, because the child only wants to recite the facts he knows, not have an exchange of information on the topic. When others start a conversation with the child about the team, expecting mutual enjoyment of a topic of shared interest, they may find themselves disappointed. The child with NLD or AD is less interested in dialogue and more interested in an audience, so conversations that turn to this topic become running monologues.

## Interest in Computers

Children with either NLD or Asperger's generally show an interest in computers and appear to be skilled in computer use. This apparent aptitude is similar to these children's appearance of having good language abilities because of their large vocabularies, in that this focus on and attention to computers has led some authors to suggest that children with NLD or AD have strength in this area (Thompson 1996). Unfortunately, without careful teaching, these children's computer skills often merely reflect their general problems with organization and planning. For example, using a computer to research and write a report can be a great help to any student. Yet while children with NLD or AD may know how to play on the computer, they are often limited by an inability to keep notes filed in a meaningful manner, to use information from certain documents in other documents, or to simply create an outline of a report. The computer becomes another place these children leave confusing and disorganized information, such as files saved in a haphazard manner, never to be found again. Without guidance, children with NLD or AD can use computers as just another area for intensive focus without much interpersonal contact. Yet with intervention, their interest in computers can indeed become a strength and a potential career.

### About Computer Use

For reasons that are not clear, children and teens with neurocognitive disorders frequently develop a special interest in computers. Although this is a growing issue in our culture across all groups of teens, looking to the Internet for "friends" and recreation can become a true compulsion in this population of kids. While use of computers and shared networks at school and home is a strength and can accelerate their learning and organizational skills, immersion in this world with no balancing of real activities and relationships is dangerous. I have seen patients who insist they have many friends, and thus no need for the interventions I may be suggesting to them and their parents, because their chat-room time is their social outlet. This is a very seductive situation for these children and teens—it is a world where you can be whomever you want without reality intruding. In this controllable world, there is no need to read facial expression or decode nonverbal cues, so unlike their experience in day-to-day life. In addition, this population is naive and far from street-smart, making them vulnerable targets.

It is also important to monitor computer time to ensure the child doesn't develop a reliance on the world of fantasy games for all social interactions; this includes real-time friendships entirely focused on these computer worlds, such as role-playing games, interactive challenge games, and sites like Second Life, where you create a personality (your avatar) and can carry on a life of sorts, buying land, developing businesses, going to parties, and even participating in sexual activity. This is not to say that parents and professionals should prohibit these activities; however, given these children's level of comfort with computers, coupled with their difficulties in social functioning and tendency to want sameness and control, it is essential that they be directed toward developing *real* friendships and maintaining a balance between fantasy and reality in their lives. It's possible to envision a frightening future where all of these children live in separate rooms, never coming out, and relying on their made-up personalities and fantasy worlds for social contact—a future we must help them avoid.

## ■ Radcliff's Story

*Radcliff loves using computers and tries to keep up with the latest developments in wireless systems. As a child, he began learning how to program, starting with simple computer languages and expanding to more complex skills. His ability to focus on one thing to the exclusion of others and to learn a series of actions that he follows precisely helped him land a job with a local computer company. He does the same thing every day—tasks involving specific programming and looking for data. He likes his job and he works independently.*

## Visual-Motor and Auditory Learning Skills

Children with Asperger's frequently exhibit skill at puzzles, and they may be adept at copying letters or numbers. This visual-motor skill can help them solve problems that are presented to them in a format that taps this strength. An assignment presented as a puzzle, or a vocabulary list presented as a game involving copying or finding hidden words, may be engaging for the child with AD.

Children with NLD rarely find solving puzzles or copying letters pleasant (and rarely is it a strength), but they often excel at remembering information they hear and respond well to music as a form of relaxation. Vocabulary words presented rhythmically or in brief stories that illustrate meaning will be more helpful to students with NLD than any visual copying activity.

## Excellent Language Acquisition

Children with either NLD or AD acquire extensive vocabularies early in life. This highly developed language acquisition allows for an entrance into social interaction and academic success. This strength is highly valuable, providing the child with praise, self-esteem, and genuine enjoyment. Yet, as discussed earlier, knowledge about language and an interest in facts provided by language are only part of any social interaction. The child who relies too heavily on this one aspect of language use soon meets with social disappointment, and the asset can become a deficit.

When a child with NLD or AD is young, between ages three and seven, his precocious "little professor" speech is seen as charming and engaging by adults and is generally ignored by peers. But by age eight or nine, his peers find this style of speech intrusive and weird. By high school, his inability to adopt the flow and rhythm of the language of his peers often leads to isolation and depression. As it is often coupled with an inability to read social cues, the style of language use these children rely on for comfort and pleasure actually becomes a barrier between them and their peers. By adulthood, this is usually less of an issue, but there are many years of rejection, isolation, and social failure between third grade and adulthood.

Children with NLD or Asperger's usually perform well on tests that measure the language they take in and the language they produce. These test scores help us understand their potential for language use, but they don't reflect their functional use of language. However, scoring well is often a source of pride for these youngsters, and successes, wherever they occur, need to be supported.

## Honesty and Respect for Rules

In general, children with NLD or Asperger's don't lie, a strength that is often refreshing for teachers and parents. The reason why they don't lie is not necessarily because they are morally superior to other children. Rather, it is most likely a result of their rigid adherence to rules and structure; they wouldn't really consider lying. They are also sensitive souls who are easily hurt by the lies of others, which they experience as incomprehensible actions. Their inability to lie may weaken by the end of middle school, and these children clearly are not immune to adolescent pressures. As teens, they may engage in manipulations of the truth and errors of omission (that is, not telling the whole truth because "you didn't exactly ask about that") that are typical of others in their age group.

Children with NLD or AD learn rules and follow them, expecting others to do the same. In fact, their need for sameness, predictability, and fairness is often a source of conflict with age-mates. But their reliance on rules and predictability and their willingness to play by the rules can in fact be a great strength, as they are trustworthy and reliable and can develop into wonderful employees.

# Weaknesses: Not Exactly Bad News

There are three main interrelated general areas of functional weakness in children with NLD or AD:

1.  Visual-spatial processing and sensory-motor integration

2.  Information processing and organizational skills

3.  Social skills and pragmatic language development

These areas will be discussed in more detail in chapters 4, 5, and 6, and interventions addressing these areas will be presented in part III of this book. For now, a general overview of these areas of dysfunction or weakness is in order.

## Visual-Spatial Processing and Sensory-Motor Integration

Visual-spatial skills are the skills that allow you to use visual information to perceive the movement of your body in the world, and to plan and execute that movement. Good visual-spatial skills allow you to judge and manipulate the world and the objects in it using information from your visual field. Examples of visual-spatial skills include the ability to walk a narrow beam or to run while accurately throwing a ball to another person. These skills require visual discrimination (perception of the differences between things), accurate perception of directions and distances, and coordination of this information with the rest of your body. They require that you note aspects or characteristics of people and things and that you understand what is the same and what is different, using your visual sense and your memories of past experiences.

It sounds complicated, and it is. Yet most of us take these skills for granted. You probably think nothing of the fact that you know the relative sizes of things. When going to pick up a stack of books, you know that they will be heavier than the lunchbox you just set down, and you'll adjust your motor movement to account for that difference. You take it for granted that you can find your way from one classroom to another in a large school. For children with NLD or AD, the visual-spatial and visual discrimination skills required to accomplish all these activities are often impaired, contributing to a natural clumsiness and frequent experiences of getting lost.

Motor skills involve the ability to direct your muscles (both large muscle groups and small muscle groups) to carry out actions directed by your brain. This is an area often affected by both NLD and AD. Normal motor skill abilities develop as part of normal growth, but in the child with NLD or AD, these abilities appear impaired from an early age. In the case histories of these children, you will often hear that, as infants and toddlers, they did not explore the world primarily through crawling or hand manipulation. Instead, they often preferred learning through verbal exchanges (such as "What's that?" games) with their parents or caretakers. This preference for activities that are not based in motor movement appears to reflect, in part, a comfort with language-based interactions that seems to remain with these individuals throughout their lives.

Motor skills include both small motor and large motor activities. Small (or fine) motor activities include such things as writing, drawing, cutting, or other finger-controlled actions, to name a few. For children with NLD, motor skills that incorporate or use visual information (visual-motor activities) are most often impaired. A child with NLD may hold a fork in an odd manner or may seem unable to spread butter on a biscuit without destroying the biscuit. Drawing is less than pleasurable for many children with NLD, and taking notes, tying shoes, and other visually based fine motor activities have a high potential for failure. This difficulty with motor activities is often less far-reaching in AD, and in fact, many children with AD actually excel in drawing. Both groups of children often experience difficulty with handwriting (including taking notes in class or copying information) or manipulating small parts of things.

Large (or gross) motor activities include such things as walking, riding a bike, running, dancing, and most team sports or athletic activities. All are similarly difficult for children with either NLD or AD. Yet some of these children have mastered and learned to enjoy large motor skill activities with patient teaching. Though these children need a longer learning period than their age-mates, practice and directed teaching have been successful in helping them acquire skills in this area of weakness.

Visual-spatial processing impacts learning in many ways. Students with NLD or AD find tasks such as handwriting, taking notes, and filling in forms and worksheets difficult at best and often impossible. Given the difficulties these children have in visual-spatial processing and visual discrimination, such seemingly simple tasks are not simple. The problem is not one of failing to understand the task or not having the knowledge to complete the task; rather, the problem is that these children have a specific disability that interferes with the processing of visual-motor and visual-spatial information.

## ■ Ari's Story

*Ari is a sweet nine-year-old girl who is in a regular third-grade classroom but who receives resource help two hours a day. She was recently diagnosed with NLD, and her family and school are trying to develop a program to help her. Everyone agrees that Ari is smart, as she has no problem discussing at length the categories of birds she keeps a log on or describing in detail every aspect of all the characters in the book series she reads voraciously. She can read above her grade level, yet when she was required to do a report on Native American housing, Ari had no idea what to do. Her teacher sent home a sheet of information, two books, and separate sheets on how to organize a report. Ari's mother sat with her every day after school, succeeding only, it seemed, in provoking Ari to tears and frustration, and feeling the same way herself. Ari couldn't (or, her mother suspected, wouldn't) write a word. She became totally stumped and unable to proceed when confronted with a blank piece of paper. Her mother became angry, and her teacher was confused. Ari could read the material, clearly was listening in class, and could answer questions about Native American homes. Why couldn't she produce any work?*

# *Information Processing and Organizational Skills*

Processing the many forms of information that you come into contact with each and every day requires many brain functions and complicated communications between brain structures. As mentioned in chapter 1, the brain relies on its interconnections to convey information accurately. In people with NLD or AD, this ability is impaired, leaving them unable to easily or quickly make sense of day-to-day tasks (like schoolwork), or personal demands (like grooming or relationships). The information goes in, but once it becomes a part of the person's cognitive processes, his ability to organize and make sense of and then use or retrieve the information becomes jumbled. This is frustrating for children with NLD or AD, and it is frustrating for their parents and teachers, as well.

## Information Processing Deficits

Ari's situation illustrates the complications and real-life effects of information processing deficits. This young girl has taken in and understands the information she has been taught on Native American housing structures. The problem is twofold: First, the information is not organized in any meaningful manner in her memory, and second, even when information is organized in some manner, she cannot easily call upon it to produce a coherent written report. In essence, the information goes in and then seems to get lost in a confusing internal filing system. For children like Ari, teachers and parents need to use specific methods that convey not only the information, but also ways to remember and organize what is taught. Given the problems these children have with visual-spatial organization and information processing, traditional methods of taking notes and outlining using pencil and paper are of little use for them. Deficits in information processing underlie a great many of the difficulties these children experience.

## Social Skills and Pragmatic Language Development

The third area of weakness, in the development of social skills and pragmatic language (practical, day-to-day language that conveys social meaning), is to some degree a result of the two areas of weakness already described. The child's difficulties with information processing and confusion in accurately comprehending the actions of others, along with the spatial, motor, and organizational problems described above, combine to create pain and anxiety for the child. Normal social interactions occur on many levels simultaneously, some overt (an obvious message is conveyed, usually through language) and some covert (a hidden message is conveyed, usually via tone, inflection, body language, innuendo, or implied meaning). Children with NLD or AD do not fully grasp these multilevel communications, missing the social cues and implied meanings that others understand.

For example, a child with NLD or AD will not understand the social convention of personal space without being directly taught to stand the appropriate distance from others when interacting with them. The child will not implicitly understand the differences in personal space that depend on degrees of relationship, for example, that you stand closer to a close friend than to an acquaintance and that you maintain a respectful distance when dealing with your principal or teacher.

These children interpret language literally, often missing sarcasm, humor, or even threats. The facial expressions and changes in tone of voice that often convey the meaning in such statements are missed by these children, who rely on the literal meaning of words to understand the communication. These misinterpretations of language may be humorous, but they can also create painful and confusing social experiences.

On the morning of her fifteenth birthday, one girl was told by her mother that her birthday was a special day and she could "do whatever she wanted today." When she arrived at school that day, she had, unbeknownst to her mother, helped herself to a large amount of candy. She had a terrible day at school. In two of her morning classes, she became upset and disruptive when her work was corrected (something that was quite unusual for her). When questioned following the second episode, she finally stated, in an offhand manner, that it was her birthday and that her mother had told her she could do whatever she wanted. She took her mother's statement literally and was upset and confused when her work was not accepted as it was, since that was the way she wanted it to be.

## The Perspective of Another Person and Pragmatic Language

In general, most children and teens with NLD or AD experience great difficulty seeing another person's perspective. This appears as a failure of empathy, a self-centered worldview that often makes them seem robotlike and cold. However, this is not the case; children with NLD or AD desire close relationships with others and feel extremely sad, even falling into depression, when their relationships fail to develop.

A central focus of any intervention program must be on teaching pragmatic language, self-observation, and the ability to adopt another person's perspective. Traditionally, children with NLD or Asperger's have participated in pragmatic language training programs, usually in a small group run by a certified speech therapist. These groups, similar to social skills groups run by licensed psychologists, focus on developing the child's ability to use language appropriately and develop behaviors that are socially acceptable. Success while in the group is usually high, and the experience is a valuable one. Yet most professionals find that the skills developed in the group do not easily generalize beyond the group. This may have to do with the child relying on context for clues to expected behaviors; as a result, when the behavior is expected out of context (outside of the pragmatic language program), it is confusing for them. It is a problem worth further study.

### Pragmatic Language Screening

At the Orion Academy, we use the following questionnaire to assess pragmatic language skills. Developed from a form used at Pathways Academy at McLean Hospital in Boston, this pragmatic language skills review is used to evaluate an entering student's current pragmatic language level. It is then used again over the years to measure improvement. Students eventually learn to rate themselves and participate in the development of their pragmatic language skills. Development of useful measures of progress in these skills is another area in need of further research.

## PRAGMATIC LANGUAGE SKILLS REVIEW

Next to each statement, please write the number that best describes the frequency of the behavior:

1 = almost always
2 = usually
3 = about half the time
4 = rarely
5 = almost never

The lower the total score, the greater the person's pragmatic language abilities.

### Nonverbal Communication

_____ 1.  Looks at the eyes of person he or she is speaking with

_____ 2.  Uses facial expressions appropriate to the content of his or her words

_____ 3. Understands the facial expressions of others and responds appropriately

_____ 4. Understands the emotions of others and responds appropriately

_____ 5. Recognizes nonverbal cues and gestures (body language)

_____ 6. Acts at an age-appropriate level

_____ 7. Recognizes the spatial relationship between people or objects and self: stands the appropriate distances from others and has sense of the size and weight of things

_____ 8. Refrains from making inappropriate noises

## Expressive Skills

_____ 1. Speaks clearly (does not mumble)

_____ 2. Speaks with varied and appropriate tone and volume

_____ 3. Is able to take another person's perspective

_____ 4. Does not get stuck on one topic, as if unaware of others' interest

_____ 5. Understands sarcasm

_____ 6. Understands and uses metaphor appropriately

_____ 7. Can let go of an argument even if the other person does not agree

_____ 8. Understands his or her own internal state and can respond to inquiries about himself or herself with more than "I don't know"

## Conversational Skills—Staying on Topic

_____  1.  Chooses a topic appropriate to the setting

_____  2.  Introduces and discusses topics clearly

_____  3.  Expresses relevant information and expresses it concisely

_____  4.  Maintains a topic in conversation

_____  5.  Changes topics appropriately

_____  6.  Understands how to tailor conversation to the audience— for example, peers versus teachers

## Conversational Skills—Turn Taking

_____  1.  Takes turns in conversation; does not monopolize

_____  2.  Attends to listeners' comprehension and attention to what he or she is saying

_____  3.  Is appropriate when interrupting both peers and adults

_____  4.  Waits to be called on or acknowledged before speaking in class or a group

_____  5.  Appropriately asks a speaker to clarify comments made

_____  6.  Is flexible when there is a change in topic

## Speech Conventions

_____  1.  Introduces himself or herself to others appropriately

_____  2.  Uses appropriate conversational pleasantries (greetings, apologies, responses to others)

_____  3.  Makes himself or herself available for conversation (is approachable)

_____ 4. Talks to people, not at them

_____ 5. Asks for help when needed

_____ 6. Initiates original (nonredundant) conversation

## Peer Skills

_____ 1. Establishes and maintains appropriate friendships

_____ 2. Refrains from making fun of others

_____ 3. Welcomes others to join in groups

_____ 4. Offers and accepts criticism appropriately

_____ 5. Offers and accepts compliments appropriately

_____ 6. Uses appropriate slang with peers

_____ 7. Demonstrates empathy

_____ 8. Seems confident in both same-sex and opposite-sex interactions

_____ 9. Responds to verbal conflicts appropriately

_____ 10. Compromises and negotiates appropriately

_____ 11. Can let others "win" arguments

_____ 12. Listens to another person's perspective without having to impose his or her own

## Other

_____ 1. Recognizes and expresses his or her own emotions

_____ 2. Does not blame others for his or her own issues or feelings

_____ 3. Demonstrates remorse when appropriate

_____ 4. Assertively deals with peer pressure

_____ 5. Respects the hierarchy of a school or other setting

_____ 6. Cares what others think of him or her

_____ 7. Can understand the purpose of rules, even when he or she doesn't agree

Although it was designed for use in a specific school setting, Orion's pragmatic language skills review is a tool that can be used by parents and professionals who know a child well. It allows parents and professionals to understand the complexity of the language skills we all use on a day-to-day basis. Further, the review sheet provides a way to evaluate the current skill level of a child and to reevaluate the child periodically, allowing parents and teachers to plan interventions that target specific areas of difficulty. Any child with NLD or AD can develop or improve his pragmatic language skills, and the involvement of the school and the family is central to the process. A tool such as the review sheet offered here is one way to increase understanding between the family and school, involving both in the support of the child.

# 3

# Why It's Important to Correctly Assess the Child with NLD or AD

A child born with nonverbal learning disorder or Asperger's disorder is not the child most parents expected. These children's needs often defy definition, and a parent's feelings of helplessness and inadequacy can increase with each passing year. This charming, loving young person seems impossible to predict at times, cannot achieve in areas other children find easy (riding a bike, tying shoes, participating in birthday parties, turning in completed homework assignments, and so on), and struggles with worries and fears that parents find difficult to understand.

These children are also not the students expected by most school districts. Neither learning disabled in the traditional sense nor classically gifted, they present a challenge teachers and schools are rarely prepared for. Many fall into the unusual category of "gifted learning disabled" (which is not the contradiction in terms it appears to be). But as the child with NLD or AD gets older, the "gifted" part of her learning disability seems less helpful. The language skills that the child relies on are not enough as the need for social skills and more complex information processing come to the fore. The child experiences school as increasingly confusing and frustrating. For most of these children, the third grade marks a point where they face a decline they cannot seem to reverse alone. Social pressures increase—everyone isn't as accepting as in first and second grade—and the academic challenges increase dramatically. For these children, success may not be the same as what's expected for their neurotypical peers; rather, it will be measured in the progress they achieve in overcoming the obstacles their learning differences present. It's important to keep in mind that progress is what matters, not perfection.

In third grade, classrooms across the country begin to expect integration of information as part of the learning process. In addition, textbooks purposely ask questions or present problems in ways different from how the material was taught. This educational trend, designed to increase flexibility in learning and thinking, can cause problems for children with NLD or AD even earlier than third grade. For example, consider a first-grader struggling with the math concept of place value. In the classroom and on the practice sheet, the word "groups" is used: "Put these apples into groups of ten. How many groups of ten do you have?" Yet on the worksheet sent home for homework, the child is confronted with problems that ask her to put the items into "sets." She is unable to do the worksheet, and her teacher is confused about how she could have forgotten this concept, when that very day she could do it in class.

However, she has not forgotten the concept. The problem is that the word "sets" does not mean the same thing to her as "groups," and thus she has no idea what is being asked of her. Her significant learning disability in processing information and rigidity of thinking contributes to her perceived failure. Although the problem in this example can be resolved with modifications to classroom materials and teaching methods, it also reflects a learning challenge that children with NLD or AD must conquer. The world will present all children with unique situations where they need to apply their knowledge in a novel manner—something that will not come easily to the child with NLD or Asperger's.

# Program Needs

As a parent, you will need to become knowledgeable about NLD or AD—not only so you understand your child's challenges and can thus help address them, but also because, ultimately, it will fall to you to become the advocate for your child. This will be the case unless or until schools recognize the great needs and vast potential of these children and begin providing an education that benefits them. As the previous chapters have suggested, such an education will need to include programming in these children's three major areas of weaknesses:

1. Visual-spatial processing and sensory-motor integration

2. Information processing and organizational skills

3. Social skills and pragmatic language development

Most school districts and, unfortunately, many uninformed professionals often misdiagnose children with NLD or AD. As a result, they misunderstand these children's needs and may provide programs that are ineffective at best and harmful at worst. Children with NLD or AD are often misdiagnosed as having some form of attention-deficit disorder, and the NLD or AD is not diagnosed. Another issue is that many children with NLD or AD also have anxiety disorders, but these are often overlooked, so treatment for the anxiety goes lacking. Issues of attention and concentration, as well as anxiety management, have a major effect on those with NLD or AD and must be considered as part of any assessment or intervention.

# Attention-Deficit Disorder

The most common error in assessing these children is to diagnose them as having attention-deficit disorder, a specific and separate disorder that has some overlapping criteria. The major categories they are misdiagnosed in are ADHD-HI (attention-deficit/hyperactivity disorder, hyperactive-impulsive type) or ADHD-I (attention-deficit/

hyperactivity disorder, inattentive type). The criteria for a diagnosis of ADHD are shown in table 3.1. The issues of impulsivity, distractibility, and poor concentration are central to this diagnosis.

---

# Table 3.1:
# Diagnosis of Attention-Deficit Disorder

Attention-deficit symptoms are present in early childhood, are behaviors that are persistent, and occur in many settings (not just at home or at school). These symptoms have been evident for at least six months, are inconsistent with the development level, and are causing significant impairment in social, academic, or occupational functioning. Onset of the symptoms occurs before age seven.

There are three categories of attention-deficit disorders:

### ADHD—inattentive type (ADHD-I)

- Does not appear to be listening

- Cannot sustain attention once he or she begins—in tasks or in play

- Makes careless mistakes and/or fails to pay attention to details

- Has trouble organizing self and activities

- Has trouble following through with assignments or tasks

- Avoids tasks with multiple steps or requiring sustained effort

- Easily distracted by outside stimuli (clocks ticking, people talking)

- Forgets what he or she is supposed to be doing

- Loses things—books, pencils, keys, toys

---

## ADHD—hyperactive-impulsive type (ADHD-HI)

- Fidgets or squirms; can't sit still

- Often appears to be on the go

- Runs around or climbs on things excessively

- Blurts out answers without being called on

- Talks excessively

- Has trouble waiting to take turns

- Interrupts or intrudes in conversation

- Seems to never be quiet

- Has trouble working alone

## ADHD—combined type (ADHD-C)

- Has characteristics of both sets of criteria

Although it is possible for a child to have both ADHD and NLD or AD, this is not necessarily the case, even when it has been suggested to a parent. In young children, NLD and AD often appear with symptoms similar to those of ADHD: concentration problems, impulsivity, and distractibility. But those very symptoms are also part and parcel of NLD and AD.

In some ways, an attention deficit functions in a neuropsychological disorder like a fever functions in a medical disorder. The fever in and of itself only indicates a problem in the body. Similarly, a deficit of attention really only describes the overt problem the child is struggling with. A fever can point to many things, from spinal meningitis to a simple cold. What a difference correct diagnosis makes, as the treatment for a cold is quite different from the treatment for meningitis. Similarly, the problems that confront the child with NLD or AD are important to understand and diagnose correctly, because what is special and also problematic about NLD or Asperger's disorder is not the same as what is at issue with attention-deficit disorder. These disorders need to be understood separately.

In children with NLD or Asperger's who are also diagnosed with ADHD, the NLD or AD is the central disorder. This distinction may seem like hairsplitting—what difference does it make if the child has one diagnosis or the other or, more to the point, what difference does it make if they have both? It can make a big difference. Failure to correctly diagnose the central disorder—NLD or AD—will result in inappropriate treatment and classroom placement. Because of their problems with on-task behavior, attention, and concentration, children with NLD or AD may be misdiagnosed as having ADHD. However, these children are not dealing with the same issues as those with ADHD, and placing them in classrooms with children with ADHD, whose behavioral problems are central and who respond best to behavior modification and stimulant medication is a serious mistake. Although medication can be helpful for some children with NLD and many with Asperger's, behavior modification techniques and classroom settings with ADHD children are not useful options. The particular pragmatic social needs of children with NLD or AD are ignored under this approach, and the anxiety they feel usually increases in these settings. Further, their visual-spatial difficulties remain untouched in favor of controlling their behavior.

## Impulsivity

Impulsivity is a tendency toward sudden action on a thought or idea without consideration of the effect that action might have. In NLD and Asperger's, the impulsivity often displayed by these children is the result of a rigid style of thinking that requires certain reactions to certain stimuli. The need to react to the stimuli is experienced as immediate, with no delay or "buffer zone," if you will, before thought becomes action. For example, if someone in a classroom mentions baseball, the impulsive child may hop out of her seat and get the baseball from her backpack to throw around the class, never thinking this will get her in trouble.

Children with NLD or Asperger's are most likely to engage in verbal impulsivity. Teachers often see this in the form of blurting out the answer to a question (right or wrong) without waiting to be called on. Other forms of verbal impulsivity relate to compulsive behaviors some of these children experience. A child might find herself repeating a word in a rhyme sequence, impulsively indulging in a string of nonsense words she finds funny. For example, if a vocabulary word is "orange," and child might repeat "orange," then proceed to say "lorange," "forange," "porange," "sorange," and on and on. Needless to say, others do not find this very funny.

## Distractibility

Distractibility is simply the tendency to become distracted—shifting attention from what one was supposed to be focusing on. Some people can actually manage to maintain attention on more than one thing at a time. Unfortunately, for those with NLD or Asperger's, this is not usually the case. For children with NLD or AD, distractibility appears to be due to heightened sensitivity to stimuli (smell, sound, feel) or to a ruminative thought stuck in the child's head. Distractibility is evident when a child looks to the clock whenever it ticks or stares at another child, unable to get back on task because the other child is tapping a pencil. This difficulty with concentration stems from a combination of all the deficits previously mentioned, together with the anxiety these children deal with on a day-to-day basis. Try paying attention to a teacher who is talking about long division when you hear the child next to you tapping a pencil, the clock ticking, and the hum of the heater—all while you try to tune out recurring thoughts about Pokemon (which you actually prefer to think about) and arrange your body at a desk that causes you to lean forward in an uncomfortable position. Most adults would be hard-pressed to stay focused on the lesson.

# Anxiety Disorders

Anxiety is a feeling of worry or fear that can occur at any time, often for no apparent reason. During most of human evolution, anxiety was necessary for survival. A cognitive appraisal of threat is a prerequisite for the experience of this emotion. The early human who experienced a sense of anxiety and was careful when hearing the growls of a saber-toothed tiger was more likely to survive (and less likely to be lunch) than the human who had no sense of what to be anxious about. When anxiety no longer functions to warn us and provide a way of accurately judging the safety of our environment, that anxiety can become the source of a disorder.

There are a number of anxiety disorders recognized in *DSM-IV*, and much research is devoted to these disorders. Pediatric anxiety disorders are one of the most prevalent forms of childhood psychopathology, affecting 20 percent of children and adolescents at some point in their lifetime (Vasa and Pine 2004). Currently, three anxiety disorders show significant overlap with NLD and Asperger's disorder: obsessive-compulsive disorder, generalized anxiety disorder (GAD), and social phobia or social anxiety disorder. As interest increases regarding the overlap, or comorbidity, between anxiety disorders and NLD and AD, we will better understand the relationship between them. For now, one thing we do know is that the issues that are specific to neurocognitive disorders also make the child more susceptible to anxiety problems.

Fear conditioning and information processing, which may be influenced by genetic factors, impact the development of normal versus pathological anxiety. Fear conditioning involves an impaired ability to accurately assess threats. This could arise from an inability to distinguish features that are important from those that are not. An example would be the inability to assess the difference between the threat of a wolf in the woods versus a wolf in a zoo. Another factor in the development of fear conditioning, one that is often seen in children with NLD or AD, is the repeated experience of misreading social cues and social events, which can result in ongoing increased arousal. Because they cannot accurately predict what will occur, children with NLD or AD must remain alert and thus live in a state of heightened arousal in social situations. This level of arousal impairs their ability to monitor potential threats and distorts their ability to know when to be anxious and when not to be. Think about this in terms of the difficulty they have in processing information. Their inability to accurately assess the dangerousness of a situation or stimuli is partially a result of errors in thinking or perception, in part due to problems with memory, and reinforced by their continued experiences of anxiety in these situations.

## Memory Problems and Anxiety

Children with NLD or AD show an attentional bias toward anxiety-producing stimuli, meaning they seem more drawn then others to notice things that make them anxious. They also appear to store more harmful emotional memories than positive emotional memories. In effect, they remember the bad things more than the good and focus on them over and over—increasing the effect these memories have on them. This memory bias has been shown to run in families, and a family history of anxiety disorders predicts this mnemonic abnormality in children (Merikangas 1999). One study found that low visual-spatial memory scores in young boys predicted increased anxiety later in life (Raine et al. 2005). Given that children with NLD usually score lowered in visual-spatial memory, this noted connection is worth further study.

## Anxiety and Social Development

As mentioned above, anxiety can play an important role in survival and adaptability. We need healthy anxiety to protect us and help us negotiate the world. Yet, when management of anxiety is disrupted, whether by experiences or genetic predisposition, it impacts a child's development in many ways, most serious being the impact on social development. This impact can be seen, starting with problems in attachment to parenting figures and other caretakers, and continuing in peer relations that can arise as early as first grade. Because social relationships are reciprocal, with a give-and-take or cause and effect, the child may experience difficult social interactions early on that are likely to lead to some of the symptoms seen in anxiety disorders. The problem is often compounded by failure to diagnose these children accurately. They continue to have negative experiences, increasing their tendency to worry and see danger and reinforcing the parental response of supporting the avoidance of social situations the child comes to dread. The anxiety that develops in the child with NLD or AD in social situations then compounds their social difficulties and increases the likelihood of unsuccessful social experiences.

## ■ David's Story

*David is twelve years old, the second of four children in his family, and is large for his age. People often mistake him for being older than he is—his size and his excellent language skills probably contribute to this common error. David is sensitive to sounds and smells, has few friends, and has struggled with writing, both the motor activity and the organizational part, for years. He tests with an above-average IQ but has not always done well in school. He was recently diagnosed with NLD and has begun attending a weekly social skills group. Yet David hides a secret from peers and adults at school, at temple, and at family gatherings that include anyone other than his immediate family. David is always worried about germs. The idea of people coughing, sneezing, or breathing on food or utensils makes it almost impossible for him to eat in public. He pretends to eat so people will leave him alone, but he rarely puts anything into his mouth. He feels an overwhelming need to wash his hands when someone sneezes or coughs, and he finds himself in the bathroom more than normal—sometimes three or four times in an hour. His parents know about his worry and tell him it's silly, that he should push those thoughts out of his head. He would if he could, but the thoughts and the sounds of coughing, sneezing,* and breathing intrude anyway. David also finds it difficult to stand too close to people. He's not sure why (and it isn't always his worry about germs), but he just feels funny when there are lots of people close to him. Sometimes his heart beats faster, and he worries he'll have a heart attack. He never has, of course, and he knows it's a silly thought, but sometimes in crowded public places he still worries it will happen.

## Obsessive-Compulsive Disorder (OCD)

Many children with NLD or AD suffer from an anxiety disorder at some point in their lives; in particular, many experience symptoms of obsessive-compulsive disorder (OCD), one of the anxiety disorders identified in the *DSM-IV*. It can occur at any time in a person's life and is not unusual in children, as earlier clinicians thought. OCD is characterized by the presence of both obsessions and compulsions to a degree that causes distress for the individual and interferes with some aspect of her life—personal, professional, or academic. Normal, reasonable worries and fears are not the concerns in this disorder.

### Obsessions

Obsessions are thoughts, ideas, or mental images that occur over and over and create a sense that the person cannot control them. These thoughts appear without warning, and once they occur, the person cannot easily get them out of her mind. Some common examples are obsessive thoughts about germs, about being contaminated, or about having an accident on the road. The visual images that accompany obsessions can involve violent or sexual material and are disturbing and distracting to the individual. Needless to say, it is hard on a child to have obsessive thoughts, and perhaps even harder for parents when their child begins to describe these thoughts. But in no way does the presence of intrusive thoughts or obsessions mean the child will act on these thoughts. Many parents have worried that the fact that their child thinks these things (for example, imagines her teacher with blood running down her face) means she will do them. There is no evidence this is the case. In fact, obsessive-compulsive children are generally less violent and more frightened than most other children are.

## Compulsions

Compulsions are the actions that the person with OCD feels compelled to perform as a result of her obsessions. They are actions these people "need" to perform over and over again; for example, washing hands after touching a doorknob. Compulsions often have a number associated with them—for example, a certain number of times that an action must be performed to prevent some disaster from happening. Many times the child with OCD does not know exactly what the disaster will be; she just has an overwhelming feeling that something bad will happen. The compulsive rituals that develop can take over the child's life, taking hours to perform and interfering with her day-to-day functioning.

## ■ Linda's Story

*Linda was an excellent student, getting grades that never went below a B. In the middle of sixth grade, she began to worry more and more about being able to maintain her academic prowess. Without knowing when it started, she found herself involved in a thinking ritual that she felt she had to do to avoid getting a poor grade on a test. This ritual consisted of thinking of every bad grade she could get, in order, without allowing a positive thought to intervene. It went like this: "I'll get an F. I'll get a D, I'm sure of it. I'll get a C." If the thought that she might get an A or a B slipped in, or if she was interrupted in this thinking series, she had to start again. As time went by, she began engaging in these thinking rituals about all her worries, especially about the safety of her mother and father. Finally, her grades began to suffer and her daily life was disrupted by the amount of time it took her to complete these rituals.*

## Treating Children with OCD

Needless to say, treatment of OCD is essential if the child is to be able to function in any school program. Most children with OCD respond very well to the standard treatments, which usually involve taking medication to lessen the symptoms while the child completes a course of cognitive behavioral therapy. John March, MD, has cowritten an excellent book describing the treatment of children with OCD: *OCD in Children and Adolescents: A Cognitive-Behavioral Treatment Manual* (March and Mulle 1998). Any parent whose child has developed symptoms of OCD, with or without NLD or Asperger's disorder, should seek competent evaluation and treatment for the child. Early intervention is more likely to be successful, and for children, many of whom do not require continued medication, the tools of cognitive behavioral therapy are effective throughout their lives. As with a dual diagnosis with ADHD, in children with NLD or Asperger's who are also diagnosed with OCD, the NLD or AD is the central disorder, and educational programs and other interventions must address this central disorder.

## Generalized Anxiety Disorder

Generalized anxiety disorder (GAD) is defined by excessive worry—worry that is beyond what would be expected for the circumstances or that carries on long past the end of the event. It is worry that affects multiple life domains, not one specific area, such as fear of flying. It is persistent over time and frequent enough that the person makes changes in her life to deal with it. The person with GAD and her family will experience the worry as difficult to control, and no matter how bright she is, using logic to control the worry doesn't help. So far the majority of the research on GAD has been on adults, but that doesn't mean children and teens are immune to this disorder. As a group, children and teens with neurocognitive disorders appear more prone to anxiety management issues. Although all may not be diagnosed with GAD or another anxiety disorder, there is definitely an overlap between anxiety disorders and neurocognitive disorders. This becomes more apparent upon review of the characteristics of GAD:

- Focus on catastrophe: In GAD, a person can become consumed with worry about almost anything. Some students at the Orion Academy have described an internal thought process they struggle with when seeing the news (print or TV) or having the focus of their worry brought up in class. It goes something like this: Increasing global warming means that the rain forests will be destroyed, which will create havoc on the planet, dooming their future. Eventually they will be homeless and the planet ruined, so why try in school? And what's the use of having friends if everything will be destroyed, anyway?

- Perfectionist thinking: If the person can't be perfect or do something perfectly, then why bother?

- Distortions of thinking and perceptions: Small errors are not accepted, and small changes are seen as major events and reason for worry.

- Self-consciousness: The child or teen needs frequent assurances. She isn't sure she is acting appropriately.

- Rigid adherence to rules: This is done in an attempt to cope and control anxiety. But in the real world there are many gray areas, and thus life often causes the person increased anxiety, as her rules are not rigidly adhered to.

- Somatic complaints: Physical complaints are common, including an increased tendency to get headaches and stomachaches and exacerbation of existing illnesses.

- Sleep disturbance: This is a common symptom of anxiety disorders as well as depression. For many children with neurocognitive disorders, sleep difficulties have been a lifelong issue.

- Irritability and concentration problems: This symptom of GAD may in fact be a result of other symptoms, such as sleep difficulties and distortions of thinking.

- Appear as "little adults": In children with GAD, this symptom seems to be an attempt at coping, but, as in NLD and AD, it is often a result of rigid thinking and a need to control the external environment.

GAD generally has a slow onset, occurring over time in such a way that parents or teachers may not notice the changes at first. As symptoms increase, the disorder may be diagnosed. According to a study by Rob McGee, a specialist in preventive medicine for children, there are no gender differences until adolescence, at which point girls are more likely to develop GAD (McGee et al. 1990). Overall, GAD is reported in 10 to 14 percent of all children, and it is a serious diagnosis, being associated with major depression, suicide, and low self-esteem. It also has a major impact on functionality.


## Social Phobia

The ability to be social is highly valued in our society. Assessing others on their sociability, ranging from outgoing to shy, is a common measurement and often implies a judgment of the person. Many children and teens with NLD or AD are seen as nonsocial—loners who seemingly prefer not to be in the company of others. Though this apparent preference can easily be viewed as resulting from social anxiety, that is not always the case. It can be a complex response to many factors, most importantly their issues with processing social information. That said, it's important to be aware of when their response to social expectations constitutes a social phobia.

Social phobia is an anxiety disorder marked by a desire for social interactions that is interrupted by a persistent, notable, and non-age-appropriate fear of social situations and interactions. Children and teens with social phobia will have these fears in most, if not all, social interactions; this means they have phobic responses frequently, even daily. The fear is more than just shyness—it's significant enough to prevent them from engaging in social interactions. When they do find themselves in social situations, they become distressed and overwhelmed and often have a panic reaction of some kind. Children and teens with social phobia generally have poor social skills, but this doesn't necessarily indicate that they have NLD or Asperger's disorder.

## School District Diagnosis vs. Clinical Diagnosis

Since the passage of Public Law 94-142 in 1975 (the Individuals with Disabilities Education Act), school districts across the country are required to provide special education services to students whose disability "prevents them from benefiting from their education." Many states have added to and otherwise modified the original law, so parents need to be knowledgeable about the laws for their particular state. Every school district also has a unique and specific set of guidelines for inclusion in special education programs. The department of education in each state can help parents get accurate information about the laws in their area.

It is important to remember that the language of the professional medical and mental health communities is not the same as that of the educational community. School districts use categories and labels that may sound like the labels and diagnoses in the *DSM-IV*, but they do not necessarily mean the same thing. The *DSM-IV* has no diagnosis for NLD, nor does it have "behavior disorder" as a diagnosis, although school districts may use that category. Similarly, school districts often refer to students as severely emotionally disturbed (SED); this, too, is not a *DSM-IV* diagnosis. Qualifying a child for special education services under the SED category usually reflects a decision by a group of people, including the parents, about the types of services that will likely benefit the child.

It can be confusing for parents when the different systems talk about their child using different language—or, worse, language that bunds the same but has different meanings. Parents must not only learn to decode the world of their child with NLD or Asperger's; they must also learn the language of the systems they interact with in regard to their child. At times, this interaction may require the help of education attorneys and other professional advocates.

It is essential that parents and education professionals become informed about NLD and AD. If the adults around children with these disorders lack the knowledge to evaluate services, plan programs, and provide a safe learning environment, the children's future looks bleak. Without the right diagnosis, incorrect services may be put in place, sometimes setting a child back years. The child with NLD or AD may be placed in a classroom with children whose needs are severe and also quite different than her needs. The last thing a child with NLD or AD needs is to be placed in a classroom with students with behavioral problems of any kind. Nor should such children be placed with children of limited intellect or language-based learning disorders.

In the right environment, these children's special talents overshadow their challenges. Through continued research into these disorders and a deeper understanding of them, we can develop successful learning environments for these children. With appropriate services and planning, children with NLD or AD can look forward to a future as bright and full of possibilities as anyone could wish for them.

# PART II

# The Effects of Nonverbal Learning Disorder and Asperger's Disorder

# 4

# Speaking a Different Language: Social Skills Development and Social and Emotional Functioning

As we saw in previous chapters, nonverbal learning disorder and Asperger's disorder affect three main areas of functioning:

1. Visual-spatial processing and sensory-motor integration

2. Information processing and organizational skills

3. Social skills and pragmatic language development

This chapter and the next two will discuss the effects NLD and AD have on each of these areas.

## Where the System Breaks Down

If one area most dramatically sets children and teens with NLD or AD apart from their peers, it is the area of social and emotional functioning. These children experience difficulties in reading subtle social cues and understanding day-to-day social conventions. They don't really understand how to fit in or be "cool." They have trouble understanding how others feel or learning to be flexible in how they present themselves to others. They seem to have missed out on developing coping strategies for the complexities of peer interactions. In short, their system of social functioning doesn't run as smoothly as most people's, and it is most likely to break down in the following three areas:

1.  Failure in the use of pragmatic language: This is a disorder in the use of practical, day-to-day language.

2.  Failure to understand and utilize the interactive quality of language: These children use language to tell others things or carry on a monologue, not to interact. They also experience significant difficulty understanding and sending appropriate social cues using voice tone, body language, humor, and innuendo or implied meaning.

3.  Failure in the ability to simultaneously track multiple levels of social interactions: This is an inability to keep track of tone of voice, body posture, gestures, and facial expression, as well as the actual meaning of the words conveyed.

Children with NLD or AD generally desire relationships. They form close attachments to their families and often have a naïveté about them that adults find endearing, though their peers can tease them relentlessly about it. Indeed, these children's social and emotional dysfunction affects every aspect of their lives and, if left untreated, is usually the reason they fail to make a transition to a separate and meaningful life outside the family. In short, social skills dysfunction is among the most serious issues confronting these children, and it is probably the most difficult to successfully overcome without professional intervention.

## A Word About Teasing

Teasing becomes the central torment for most children with NLD or AD. It is the reason parents most often cite for seeking new programs for their children. While most children and teens with NLD or AD appear normal in most physical aspects, their peers know they are different and react to this difference. This reaction from others, combined with the child's limited repertoire of responses, often sparks escalating unpleasant interactions. Their incredibly poor social skills, combined with their desire to use language as a solution to their problems and a cover when they are uncomfortable, makes for a bad mix with other kids. Every one of the many children I have worked with complains about being teased, and they all dream of a place where they can be accepted and make friends. Unable to find a way out of the cycle of being teased, they usually withdraw into increased depression and isolation. Early attempts to fight back by engaging their peers in verbal exchanges are usually glaringly unsuccessful, adding confusion and humiliation to the mix. Eventually, these children find themselves on the periphery of social events, ever circling, never involved.

Although the stories these children tell are heartrending, it is important not to overreact and remove them from all contacts that might prove to be unpleasant. Protecting them from insensitive peers and moving them to safe and controlled environments doesn't ultimately solve the problem. Such an intervention has a place and can be an appropriate part of an overall plan. But children with NLD or AD must learn coping skills and, even more important, must come to understand their part in social interactions if they are ever to create the friendships and working relationships they desire. They will never be able to control other people, only themselves. This alone is a hard lesson for these children and teens, who often see control, logic, and "fairness" as the basis of all interactions. But the rest of the world may not see life as they do. The sooner they learn ways they can change their part of an interaction, the sooner they will be successful in the world. Their particular disabilities clearly impact learning this skill; as we have seen, these children have a very hard time understanding the complexities involved in social interactions, and they have an even harder time understanding how they contribute to their own social problems. A focus on creating change in several areas of language and social behavior will be necessary to improve the child's ability to interact and cope with others. This will be discussed at length in chapter 10.

## ■ Andi's Story

*Andi is a ten-year-old girl who is a fourth-grader at a local public school. She tries very hard in her class and wants to have friends, but to her it seems the other girls have a secret language she doesn't understand. When she tries to talk to them about a book she is reading or about cats, a favorite subject of hers, they listen politely for a few minutes and then start talking about something else. She has tried telling them more about cats or books in the hopes of interesting them with her knowledge, but it doesn't seem to work. They often walk away from her, and no one seeks her out to talk to or play with. Teachers and students notice Andi's monotone style of speech, but they aren't sure what to say about that—and Andi has no idea what people mean when they do try to describe it to her.*

Children with NLD or AD often fail to make language work for them in social situations. For example, consider this situation: Mrs. Wong (a teacher) has asked Sue (a fourth-grader with NLD) to be in charge of the coveted red, bouncy ball at recess. Sue, not really understanding the potential for social status presented to her here, will likely respond by giving the ball to whomever asks for it first. Instead of including herself in the play and becoming part of the group of children, she is likely to hover and worry, keeping track of the "rules" for use of the ball. Without help, she is unlikely to know how to organize any play with the ball, not to mention how to keep herself involved. As we will discuss later in this book, children with NLD or AD may not be adept at sports or activities using motor skills, whether gross or fine, but with direction and help they can be involved in play—as referees, organizers, and scorekeepers. The key is in helping them learn how to turn a deficit into an asset.

# Failure in the Use of Pragmatic Language

Language is a comfort for children and teens with NLD or AD, and they rely on it, even hiding in their words at times. They tend to produce a lot of language, but it fails to work for them in a number of important ways.

- They produce language that is accurate but not functional. It conveys information but fails to establish connections between the child and others.

- They understand the content of the words but often miss the emotional implications language can have. In particular, they tend to overlook the potential emotional impact their words can have on others, although they may feel the impact others' words have on them.

- They talk at people, not with them. This behavior is a direct result of their inability to realize that language is a way of interacting, not just lecturing. A monologue on whether an ion cloud has a circle shape or an oval shape may be interesting to a science teacher, but to other adolescents it is boring and pedantic.

- They fail to understand the nuances of language, focusing on concrete interpretations of what others say. Oliver's story, in chapter 1, illustrates this problem: Oliver understands the teacher's message that he "does not want to see" him playing with the toy as a message to remove the toy from the teacher's line of sight rather than to put it away, as was implied by the teacher's statement.

- They have difficulty with sarcasm or humor, since humor often relies on tone and inflection of speech for its effect. This problem makes negotiating the social hierarchy of middle school or high school almost impossible for many of these children.

Additionally, their prosody, or the tone and rhythm of their speech, is often significantly off. Again, they have trouble with the subtleties that make language more than an act of speaking, and they fail to understand that how you say something can be as important as what you say. Take the phrase "Mrs. Lee, do you want me to read this book now?" Where you put the inflection conveys as much as the literal meaning of the words. Here are a few examples:

- "Mrs. Lee, do you want *me* to read this book now?" (Not me; surely you must mean that other kid over there.)

- "Mrs. Lee, do you want me to read *this* book now?" (Not this book; you must mean another book.)

- "Mrs. Lee, do you want me to read this book *now*?" (What? This very minute?)

There are other possible inflections, but the point is clear: Each sentence, although it contains the same words, has a different meaning. In fact, a couple of these statements, if said in the manner suggested, would appear rude to a teacher or other adult in authority. The child with NLD or AD has not learned the nuances of the variations presented here, and would need these examples explained.

And finally, the good memory these children often have may actually be a detriment in social situations, as they tend to rely on rote fact. When in a stressful situation (as almost all social situations are for the child with NLD or AD), they will tend to talk about something that makes them comfortable. This is likely to be an area of special interest or knowledge they have spent time learning about. It is also likely to be something unusual or very detailed. Unfortunately, this response can worsen the situation, as peers and others will usually find the conversation boring and lose interest in continuing the interaction. The child will have a difficult time understanding that his audience has lost interest in the topic. Teenage peers may also make sarcastic comments, or ignore the teen with NLD or AD, which is hard for him to understand. By the same token, these children do not make very good listeners when someone else is talking about topics they are not interested in. They usually need specific and direct teaching on how to engage in the give-and-take of appropriate social conversation.

# Failure to Understand the Interactive Quality of Language

Failure to understand and utilize the interactive qualities of language may be, in many ways, the single most devastating disruption that results from NLD and AD. There is a growing body of literature on the concept of theory of mind, which refers to having the capacity to understand that others have desires, intentions, and beliefs that differ from one's own. In his book *A History of the Mind* (1999), author Nicholas Humphrey describes the difference between the mind and the brain and the difficulties in thinking about thinking. This line of thought is further explored by Simon Baron-Cohen in his essay *Mindblindness* (1995), an important work that helps us understand that the inability to adopt another person's perspective underlies the majority of the social difficulties children with NLD or AD experience. These children fail to recognize the point of view of others, or even to realize that others have a point of view that influences their behavior. It follows, then, that they don't realize that what they do affects the thinking—and thus the behavior—of others. They don't really know that others even experience feelings about them (except for the most demonstrative forms of anger or joy). This failure occurs at the most basic level of human interactions, the connectedness we feel with each other.

## How Relationships Form

The ability to have meaningful relationships with others is based in part on shared experiences—a sense that you and the other person are of like mind. This connected feeling develops early in life through normal interactions, with no direct teaching. Language helps form this sense of social connectedness, but most of us experience it long before we have acquired spoken language. For normally developing young children, much is conveyed in body language, gesture, facial expression, and eye gaze. Even children too young to talk will point and look at an object, directing their caregiver to look in that direction.

This nonverbal direction involves a complicated series of interactions and has as a basic premise the child's understanding that both he and the other person are thinking—and thinking about the same thing. It is an amazing and complicated process, and it's also something we take for granted every day. Not so for kids with NLD or AD. This skill is something they never really master, and as a result, all their advanced language skills fail to allow them into this secret club of mind reading—for to them such nonverbal communication must seem like a psychic ability.

## Theory of Mind

Simon Baron-Cohen (1995) discusses at length the concept of theory of mind, which involves the common human ability to "mind read." Of course what he describes isn't really mind reading (as in late-night advertisements for psychic hotlines); instead, it is the ability to read others and develop a good idea of what they are thinking. This ability manifests itself when we follow the line of a conversation or read a gaze or gesture and assume that we share ideas about what things mean. For example, we assume that when we describe something as "red," the other person holds the same idea of red as we do. Indeed, if the other person is color-blind, this would not be true, so there are times when our assumptions about shared thinking are incorrect.

Theory of mind allows us to hold in our minds a full range of mental representations: "Dog" is a specific mental representation; "car" is a different mental representation. Further, and in many ways more importantly, theory of mind also describes our ability to develop a "theory" about thinking. This means we understand that other people believe or think things—an understanding that is a must if one is to decode social behavior in any useful or meaningful manner.

We see theory of mind operating in the ability to do many things:

- Pretend

- Understand what a dream is

- Apply beliefs to understanding emotions

- Distinguish appearance (what something looks like) from reality (what something is)

- Introspect (demonstrate an awareness of one's own thought)

- Develop the executive function (disengage from current action to change or formulate plans, or take action on those plans)

- Integrate information

Children who do not develop these skills will have to be directly taught to understand the feelings and beliefs of others, learning socially appropriate responses along the way. This applies to children with NLD and many children with Asperger's. The failure of people with NLD or AD to understand the interactive qualities of language can be understood as a deficiency in their theory of mind—they cannot "mind read." The effects of that disability manifest in many ways, a number of which have already been described, but let's take a closer look at how a deficiency in theory of mind can affect interactions with others:

- When they engage others in conversation, these children's narratives are often disjointed, out of context, superficial, or otherwise confusing. But they know just what they mean and have difficulty appreciating that others do not understand them.

- These children tend to have areas of interest or idiosyncratic focus; these are often called "enthusiasms." The child will often launch into a monologue on the subject and is not likely to notice that his listener has lost interest in the topic.

- As mentioned before, these children may often speak in a monotone or have a bland tone of voice. This may be because they lack the concept that the listener may be interested and that they could make their speech sound interesting. In effect, they are not speaking for or to the other person, but more to themselves; the idea of keeping someone interested is a novel concept.

- These children never really understand the concept of pretending. They are unlikely to engage in a lot of fantasy play or "pretending" as young children, especially when pretending involves engaging others in the fantasy. For many, engaging in mutual pretend play would be very difficult, as it requires a shared imagining, or thinking together. Keep in mind that this is not the same thing as playing computer fantasy games. Those role-playing games are not generated by the child's own imagination; rather, these game draw the child into a world of rules set out by other people for the game; once you learn the rules, it's a very predictable world. This is not true imaginative exchange.

- In some cases, the child will have difficulty recognizing someone they have met many times before, especially if the child meets the person in a different setting than usual. For example, the private psychologist for one of the students at Orion was visiting the school, and when the student happened by, his doctor said hello to him by name. The student turned to his doctor and said, "Who are you?"

- Often, these children experience difficulty with introspection—looking inward at the self. Although these kids have the language to describe the inner world of their thoughts and feelings, they often do not have an awareness of this world. Even with direct teaching, children with NLD or AD will only slowly learn the nuances of their inner experiences.

Children with NLD or AD have significant difficulty understanding social cues. Given their inability to adopt another person's perspective or to think about how they affect others, it is no surprise that they have trouble socially. Understanding the meaning of other people's behavior is quite a task when you must work without the tools the rest of us came by naturally. An intact theory of mind involves much more than just forming connections with others. It involves complicated mental processes that can be seen working in many crucial social behaviors and skills.

## Joint Attention Behaviors

Even before they develop language, children will direct the attention of their caretakers with the direction of their gaze. Caretakers monitor the gaze of the child, and the child monitors the gaze of the adult; this means each is aware of what the other is looking at. As motor skills increase, the child will add pointing as a means of directing the visual attention of others. These joint attention behaviors are not taught; they develop naturally.

Here's an example of how joint attention behaviors work: The child sees some balloons and points toward them. Then the caretaker looks in the direction the child points, "mind reading" the intent of the child, which is to direct the caretaker's gaze toward an object. This example illustrates a showing behavior, which involves showing things to others—in essence, sharing the experience of looking at an object. Children who do not engage in joint attention behaviors, such as gaze monitoring or showing behaviors, probably have not developed the essential internal mental concept of the connectedness between themselves, their caregivers, and desired third objects (such as the balloon in the example just given). This internal concept (or set of concepts) helps form the foundation of intuition, a necessary part of "mind reading," as Dr. Baron-Cohen calls it: the power to quickly know things related to others without rationally thinking them through. Most children with NLD or AD understand the idea of seeing or looking but not the idea of knowing in the sense of intuition. The experience of knowing something implies an internal, nonverbal intuitive sense and is often difficult to define. The child with NLD or AD has significant trouble with this concept.

## Predicting the Actions and Emotions of Others

In practical terms, if you don't understand what others are thinking about and that they think about you, you cannot predict their actions. You have no idea how to affect another person's behavior. It makes the world feel random and frightening. It makes every encounter a potentially novel experience—and remember that these children suffer a disruption in their ability to integrate information (or learn) from novel situations. As we have seen, it is likely this is a real dysfunction of the brain. The rest of us learn from past experiences, building up our banks of social knowledge. These children don't, and as a result, their experience of social interactions must feel overwhelming and unpredictable. It probably feels like everyone speaks a language they don't understand and can't seem to learn. That experience of the world is likely to contribute to these kids' reliance on their own ordering systems, odd or compulsive as they may be.

Studies of the ability to predict emotions in others (versus the ability to only recognize emotions in others) have suggested that a child must understand the causes of emotions in order to predict them. The child must also have some theory about the beliefs held by the other person in order to understand what that person's emotions are. Predicting emotions is a complex skill, and one that appears to be lacking in many children with NLD or Asperger's. The consequences of this lack are easy to imagine: As with the inability to predict the actions of others, without the ability to predict the emotions of others, every social encounter would be a novel experience, an experience where you would have no idea what to expect.

# Failure to Track Multiple Levels of Social Interactions

Most of us take for granted that we can keep track of the content of a conversation, the body language and tone of voice of the speaker, and our own reaction to what is being said, all at the same time. Yet if any of these abilities were missing, imagine the many ways a simple conversation could go wrong. Now imagine how it would affect others' social acceptance of you if most of your conversations were to go wrong. That is the reality for children with NLD or AD. Because these children are likely to have difficulty reading the facial expression or tone of voice of others, they are likely to focus on concrete interpretations of the language of the speaker. This concrete or literal interpretation is what the child with NLD or AD is most comfortable tracking, but it not always what the other person means. Unfortunately, those with NLD or AD have no way of gauging that they have missed the point. When stressed, they are likely to rely on what they know—language—and continue to talk whether the other person is interested or not. Interactions go from bad to worse as the person with NLD or AD becomes confused and frustrated, starts talking more, and then experiences ridicule or rejection from the other person. Eventually, these children withdraw from any social situation they can, and their skills diminish further.

## Adolescence

When kids with NLD or AD enter adolescence and attempt to deal with the complications of adolescent social structures, they don't stand a chance. They are unlikely to have the knowledge of and experience with social interactions and "mind reading" that most of us have. These teens' point of view is self-focused, and their inability to adopt the perspective of another person further contributes to them being totally unaware of the rules of social conduct. Over my years of working specifically with this age group, I've identified a number of specific issues that are important to address, as detailed below.

- **Lack of self-reflection:** As a group, adolescents with NLD or AD manage to grow chronologically, reaching the age of fourteen to eighteen, without achieving an equal growth in maturity, particularly in the ability to honestly evaluate themselves. The distortions they perceive about others are often mirrored in simplistic and immature reflections about self. This difficulty can be addressed in both a school setting that incorporates social development, self-awareness and personal advocacy into the day-to-day program and in therapy, if the teen is open to change. If they don't address this issue, and the others that follow, the future catches them unaware and unprepared.

- **Denying the future:** You might think of this as the Scarlet O'Hara school of thought: "Tomorrow is another day." These teens resist planning for the future, instead maintaining pat responses or simplistic ideas of what they will do after high school. As one student told me as he began his senior year, "Next year, I'm going to take a year off." I could only think, "A year off from *what?*" He didn't know; this was just the line he had come up with because he and his parents really weren't sure what was next for him. Although difficulty planning for the future is an issue for many teens, including those not affected by NLD or AD, those with neurocognitive disorders will need more planning and very structured support to make the transition to adulthood successful. They cannot afford to ignore the future. The fact that this is such an issue in this population of kids is, in all likelihood, a result of the problems they have managing anxiety; denial functions as an attempt to avoid fears related to not knowing what will come next.

- **The tendency to see one's self as less weird than others and to deny social and learning issues:** Often supported by families, this trait can result in increasing depression and contribute to a fear of the future. This is a difficult problem for professionals and families to deal with. No one wants to be the one to say to a kid, "Look, you really *are* very odd" or to make an issue of how different they are from NT (neurotypical) peers. Yet, in many cases, the desire to deny their social and learning issues sets them up to avoid seeking services and support and adds to a sense of loneliness. This denial also tends to push them away from the very people who are most like them and most likely to really *like* them—other teens with NLD or AD. This is unfortunate, as young adults with NLD or AD often report that loneliness is the hardest part of their adult lives.

■ **Increased social isolation and a reliance on computers:** As discussed earlier, the world of computers and the Internet is a seductive world for these teens. In this world, there are far fewer social cues, and those that do exist generally occur in a written form, and thus present fewer social complexities; this also allows time to process information. Teens with NLD or AD are often drawn to this world as a refuge from the pressures of real life and as a place they can engage in a fantasy life. It is very important that parents of these teens continue to push them to participate in real interactions and limit the time they indulge in this escape. For many of these kids, it can become an obsession and even an addiction. The key is balance, and as with anything that can be good in moderation but dangerous when overindulged in, life in the world of computers and the Internet needs to be balanced with real life.

Though these are some difficult challenges, don't despair. All is not lost. Teens with NLD or AD are capable of learning the rules of social conventions and developing meaningful and lasting relationships, and the earlier they begin the better. To allow these teens to grow into adulthood unprepared for the expectations of adult life is truly to abandon them to a harsh reality. Even though they have NLD or AD, they still need to learn the same lessons in life that their peers do—some easy, some hard. In many ways, developing an understanding of social interactions is one of the most important lessons to be learned. Hard as it may be, this must be part of any educational program that helps teens with NLD or Asperger's develop their special talents and become functioning members of the adult community.

# 5

# Lost in Space: Visual-Spatial Processing and Sensory Integration

People with NLD or AD have difficulty knowing the limits and extent of their physical self in the world. It is as if they are not completely aware of where their bodies begin and end. This disruption of perception is particularly acute in the areas of visual-spatial processing and sensory integration.

## Visual-Spatial Problems

As noted in chapter 2, visual-spatial processing is the ability to use information from the visual field to understand the world around you. Visual-spatial processing deficits affect how information gained through the visual field makes it into memory. For many people, remembering things they see is easier than remembering things they hear. Yet for children with NLD or AD, information gained through the visual field is less likely to make it into memory because visual-spatial processing deficits interfere. Information gained through auditory channels—listening—is more likely to make it into memory.

Visual-spatial processing problems also appear to greatly affect fine and gross motor skills, including writing, athletic ability, balance, and coordination. It is unclear why this is so, although sometime in the future, medical science may discover the reason children with NLD or AD generally experience disruption in motor development and have less muscle tone than others their age. Their poor muscle tone may be the source of their clumsiness, poor balance, coordination problems, and difficulty doing tasks that involve manipulating small objects (for example, tying shoes, threading beads, and handwork such as crochet). Poor muscle tone also tends to contribute to an odd, uneven, somewhat hunched-over manner of walking and can create problems with posture when sitting at a desk.

Visual-spatial processing helps you make choices about where or how to move or how close to or far away from an object you should be. Children with NLD or AD experience deficits in this ability that clearly contribute to their sense of being "lost in space." In fact, these children actually get lost at times, even between one part of their school and another. The fact that most of us rely on visual information to remember directions should help us understand the significance of these deficits. Malls, bus stations, doctors' offices, and parks can be very intimidating if you can't remember your way from one place to another.

## Dysgraphia

Dysgraphia, an impaired ability to write, is a common characteristic of NLD and AD. For some students, this disability will be the only obvious problem in their academic functioning and may be the reason they qualify for special education services. This problem is less of an issue when the child is allowed to use a computer, yet there often remains significant difficulty committing ideas to written words, whether by hand or with a keyboard. This difficulty appears to involve a deficit in executive function, which will be covered in chapter 6.

### Motor Skills

Most children with NLD or AD experience difficulty moving smoothly through the world: They often bump into things, jostle others in hallways, and have trouble perceiving the boundaries around their own bodies. They drop or spill things more than other children, and this experience of repeated failures and embarrassment can add to their anxiety, increasing the likelihood of another mishap.

As toddlers, these children are less likely to exhibit exploratory behaviors; instead, they use language to explore. This reluctance to use motor activities and rely instead on language is often a lifelong tendency. It is important to recognize these problems early. The child need not be resigned to a life of poor coordination and few physical activities. Practice and structured instruction, even for things other children may find natural, can make a big difference and are likely to be required. Riding a bike, tying a shoe, writing, being able to use public transportation—all are necessary for an independent life. Finding a balance between struggling to master difficult skills that don't come naturally and developing compensation techniques is the key. For some individuals, repeated practice will be needed, along with a measure of maturity and the willingness to persevere in the face of frustration.

## Sensory Integration

Sensory integration is the ability to organize the sensations of day-to-day life. It is a neurological function that occurs at the brain level, usually without thinking about it. Normally, the brain receives messages from many sources of sensory experience—what we see, smell, feel, taste, and hear from the environment around us. At the same time, we receive internal messages, too: how hungry we are, how hot or cold, what our muscles are doing, where our body is in relation to other people or objects, and information about our other body functions. Our brain integrates these messages and organizes and prioritizes them—at least, that is what is supposed to happen.

When the ability to integrate sensory information goes wrong, a person's ability to interact with the environment is disrupted. For example, a child with sensory-motor problems may have trouble walking up or down stairs. Such a child will often use the railing for support or walk one step at a time to maintain balance.

The human body uses three fundamental sensory systems: tactile, vestibular, and proprioceptive. The tactile system provides information about the texture, size, shape, and function of objects. Among many other things, it allows us to determine whether a touch is threatening or nonthreatening. In the vestibular system, the inner ear provides information about gravity, balance, and the position of one's head and body in relation to the ground—in essence, information about whether the person is standing, sitting, walking, or lying down, and whether balance can be maintained in those positions. In the proprioceptive system, joints and muscles provide information about where the various parts of the bodies are and what they are doing. For optimum functioning, these three sensory systems must work well and in concert with each other.

## Sensitivity to Sound, Touch, and Visual Stimuli

A common problem for children with NLD or AD is sensitivity to sound, touch, and visual stimuli. Ranging from severe to mild in intensity, this problem can create significant disruption in everyday functioning. For many of these children, hearing people talking in a classroom is so annoying as to be painful; touch that is intended as nonthreatening (a hug, for example) can be experienced as threatening; and colorful and exciting visual stimuli can be overwhelming and distracting. These responses to sensory information can interfere with their learning and can create behavioral responses that add to the child's sense of not fitting in.

The Tomatis Method and Tomatis Listening Therapy are two ways that sensory integration deficits can be addressed. Developed from the work of Dr. Alfred Tomatis, an otolaryngologist and researcher into the impacts of occupational noise, these methods are useful with Asperger's and NLD as well as other learning disabilities. They focus on auditory sensitivities and assist the child in developing better listening skills, tolerance for auditory input, and calm in the face of sensory overload. The Tomatis Method and Tomatis Listening Therapy are practiced by speech therapists and occupational therapists who have completed specific training in this approach.

## ■ Isabella's Story

*Isabella is a middle school girl with NLD who has significant sensory integration problems. While she is sitting in class, every sound other students make seems amplified times ten, and the sounds of everyday classroom life—the clock ticking and the sound of the pencil sharpener—all feel grating and annoying. As the day progresses and she tries to block these sounds out of her mind, she becomes increasingly irritable and distracted. One day, she yelled at a classmate who was chewing gum, "Just stop that!" Isabella was asked to leave the class, which made her feel humiliated and angry. Furthermore, she hadn't focused on any of the lesson that day, and she was falling further and further behind academically.*

### *Arousal States*

Children and teens with NLD or Asperger's disorder have difficulty maintaining a constant or balanced level of arousal. Arousal refers to attention, concentration, and a general sense that the sensory systems of the body are working together. Optimal arousal is neither too high (overstimulated, hyper, agitated) nor too low (drowsy, distracted, no information going in). With NLD and AD, children experience arousal states that are too high or too low, and as a result they have problems with attention, concentration, and behavior that interfere with learning. An excellent program used in occupational therapy, called the Alert Program (Williams and Shellenberger 1994), can help anyone become more aware of internal states and arousal. This system (which we will not deal with here) is often helpful for children with NLD or AD

Interventions for children with NLD or AD will be discussed in part III of this book. Specific interventions for visual-spatial problems and sensory integration are best dealt with by an experienced occupational therapist skilled in programs such as the Alert Program or the Tomatis Method. Appendix A offers suggestions for developing a team to plan and provide services for the child with NLD or AD.

# 6

# Roots of the Matter: Information Processing and Organizational Problems

On any given day, each of us engages in a complex series of mental tasks just to get out the door in the morning. We automatically carry out our morning routines (grooming, dressing appropriately for the event and weather, and getting food and perhaps coffee). We often help other family members complete their routines, gather what we need for the day, and carry out the motor activities that allow us to leave the house and get about our business. At times, this process goes more smoothly than at other times, but all in all we are able to multi-task, carrying on simultaneous activities with limited effort. We also make many decisions about what to do, when to do it, and what is more or less important. Some of these decisions are small (sugar or no sugar in my coffee?), others larger (if I leave in ten minutes, I might be late; should I delay or not?). This process of carrying out multiple and sometimes simultaneous activities, both mental and physical, occurs over and over again each day.

# Executive Function

A morning routine is an example of a series of behaviors a person has come to do more or less automatically. Throughout the day and throughout our lives, we establish many of these routines. They allow us to function on more than one level at a time; for example, while making coffee, you can also review your day in your head and mentally prepare yourself for what you need to do next. This ability is just one part of a set of cognitive skills described as executive function—higher order, or more complicated, thinking skills that govern many different mental processes, such as language processes, cognitive processes, and motor processes. Executive function is thought to be under the control of the frontal lobe of the brain. In simple terms, executive function encompasses the following skills:

- Formulating plans

- Taking action on those plans

- Delaying action when need be

- Operating on multiple levels

- Integrating information from one level to another (For example, while fixing coffee and thinking about upcoming meetings that day, you realize you have little coffee left and add a stop to buy coffee to your plan for the day.)

# Routines and Rigid Thinking

For individuals with NLD or Asperger's disorder, executive function appears to be less than reliable. Although the establishment of routines is something that's comfortable for most people with NLD or AD, they must rigidly adhere to these routines. They also have significant difficulty with multitasking and with integrating new information and acting on it appropriately.

In day-to-day life, we rely on flexibility and spontaneity to successfully interact with others, varying our routines as needed to fit the situation. This ability to shift thinking, to read the situation and revise plans accordingly, is significantly disrupted in those with NLD or AD. In essence, children with these disorders rely on a series of learned responses and have difficulty generalizing from one situation to another. They seem to carry around an ever-increasing collection of internal scripts that help them order their world and know how to respond. In some ways, it is as if they have to translate the information in the world into a code or language they understand before they can come up with a response that seems appropriate. This is not a very efficient system, and as the demands of day-to-day life become more complicated, the potential for error and problems increases.

## Information Storage: The Dresser Drawers

In children with NLD or AD, impairment in executive function affects planning, judgment, and overall social fluidity, and it also affects the child's ability to organize and integrate information for learning. For learning to occur, three things must be in place: attention, memory, and executive function. Learning requires that ideas and bits of information be assigned a category in the brain. It's sort of like putting your clothes into your dresser drawers; it's easy to find what you need when all the T-shirts are in one drawer, the underwear in another, and so on. (Unless you're my son, but that's another story.) These categories store information at two levels: short-term memory and long-term memory. While we're learning new information, the area where attention and memory overlap is called the working memory. Only a certain amount of information can be stored in working memory; this is also a relatively short-term area, and information can easily be lost from working memory. Executive function deficits that cause problems with planning and sequencing limit the usefulness of working memory, as irrelevant information may take up space in this storage area, sequences may be lost, and important information may not make it to long-term memory.

# Slow Processing Speed

In a dresser, each drawer contains specific things decided upon by the owner. Yet in the process of learning, a concept or fact may fit into many different categories. The most effective system of organizing concepts or facts allows easy recall while at the same time making connections between related ideas. Without such an internal organization system, it will take longer to find information and confusion easily sets in. This may be part of the reason why children with NLD or Asperger's suffer slow processing speed: it takes longer for them to access the information they need to work problems, respond to directions, or complete activities. Their need for more time is difficult for teachers and parents to deal with, as they seem to be choosing to move in slow motion. Nothing could be further from the truth. The child with NLD or AD feels increasing internal pressure to move quickly, yet cannot find the information he needs so he'll know what to do next.

The unreliable and disorganized information storage system these children function with makes their working memory less helpful to them and thus makes the transfer of information to long-term memory inconsistent. For example, consider learning about German shepherds. The primary category for organizing information about German shepherds might be "dog." While this is true—German shepherds are indeed dogs—it is a limited way to categorize or think about a German shepherd; these dogs have many unique and specific attributes, including a history of public service, and they are very different from pugs, which are also dogs.

Creating limited and rigid sets of thinking limits the child's capacity for integrative thinking—the ability to create meaningful links between bits of information. This problem is often first noticed around the third grade, when the curriculum begins to demand the ability to organize and integrate information from multiple sources rather than just reciting and remembering rote information. Activities such as writing a report or an essay are usually difficult for children with NLD or AD, as their deficits in executive function and their other learning problems come to the foreground. The process of planning, ordering information, and, most critically, carrying out a project from start to finish becomes an almost impossible task.

## Metaphor, Analogy, and Humor

Without direct intervention, children with NLD or AD experience significant difficulty understanding metaphor and analogy. Doing so requires understanding how one thing can stand for another, or seeing the links between ideas. This skill seems to develop naturally. It is more highly developed in some people, but it is not usually the result of direct instruction. Although children with NLD or AD love words and use them without hesitation, analogy and metaphor do not come easily for them. Given their cognitive rigidity and tendency to focus on the wrong detail, it's easy to see why analogy or metaphor may be difficult for them to process. Difficulties in understanding and participating in humor may have related causes. As mentioned in chapter 4, many of these children and teens have trouble understanding and appropriately participating in the humor of their peers. This inability to joke along with peers only adds to their social isolation and sense of not fitting in.

### *Homework and Other Classroom Challenges*

The problems children with NLD or AD have with organization play out in obvious ways in their scholastic lives. They rarely keep organized binders, nor do they get their assignments written down consistently. Papers and homework are lost, and reports and projects are disorganized jumbles of information that are rarely completed without significant parental intervention and many tears. Their deficits in executive function create real and persistent problems in their ability to create a personal organization system. As the demands of school increase with each grade, these children become teens who struggle and are unable to benefit from the traditional academic environment. Taking notes while listening to a lecture—which requires a high degree of multitasking—is close to impossible for these students.

Specific interventions are required if they are to succeed in the academic arena. Anger and punishment are unlikely to create positive results but neither is reducing our expectations of these children the answer.

## Focus on the Wrong Detail

Children with NLD or AD tend to focus on specific details and organize those details within rigid and limited categories. In the German shepherd example, a child with NLD or AD may focus only on the fact that the German shepherd is a dog. Yet if the teacher is presenting a story about World War II and the development of alternative methods of search and rescue (the use of these dogs being but one such method), the child may miss the point entirely and remember the story as being about a dog. Focusing on the wrong detail creates significant problems in comprehension for these children—problems that can baffle their teachers, as they see children with high vocabulary and reading levels who don't seem to understand what they are reading.

Focusing on the wrong detail affects a child's ability to read between the lines, a skill most people acquire without any direct teaching. If you focus on the wrong detail of a lesson or social situation, you miss the nuances of meaning. You also are likely to misunderstand the action or response required from you.

## Novel Situations

Problems with organization and rigid thinking also affect the ability of children with NLD or AD to adapt to novel situations. Whether this is a result of frontal lobe dysfunction (as mentioned in chapter 1) or failure to develop an adequate theory of mind (as discussed in chapter 4), these children have significant difficulty calling on past experiences and integrating that information with new circumstances to form a new plan of action. They are more likely to repeat a routine they know, almost as if they are following a script.

When the old script doesn't work, or when there is no script for the situation, the child or teen with NLD or Asperger's may experience a shutdown of sorts. This is very likely to occur when they encounter a situation that is overwhelmingly confusing and new.

These shutdowns are often the source of the behavior problems, few as they may be, that are associated with the child with NLD or AD—tantrums, refusal to work, or avoidance behaviors, such as leaving the room, putting his head down on his desk, or becoming "tired" and wanting to sleep. The child has no way to cope with a new situation that his existing mental routines cannot organize. When it's clear the child is reacting to a novel or confusing situation, his behavior should not be considered defiant or oppositional. This is not to say that behavior problems should be accepted or encouraged, nor is it to suggest that the child should be protected from novel or potentially complex situations. Instead, a learning plan with many opportunities for the child to increase his flexibility and add to his repertoire of experiences is essential. This approach, which will be discussed in chapter 10, will help the child develop a greater fund of information and lessen the likelihood that new situations will be seen as overwhelming.

## Information Processing Deficits

As mentioned earlier, it is in many ways unfortunate the name non-verbal learning disorder has been attached to this group of children. The effects of both NLD and AD appear to be more a core deficit in information processing than a disability in learning, per se. In both disorders, the disruption of organizational and planning skills is far-reaching and touches both social interaction and academic learning (for detailed lists of these impacts, see appendix D). Their difficulties understanding cause and effect and anticipating the consequences of their actions can cause teachers or peers to conclude that children with NLD or AD are deliberately violating rules or social norms. This is not the case, but without intervention, these children have no way to even explain what the problem is. Once again, it as if they are speaking a different language than everyone else.

Here are some of the most problematic aspects of this deficit in information processing:

- Difficulties in planning, organizing, and integration of thinking affect all areas of functioning.

- Difficulties taking action and following through with problem solving affect both academic and social functioning.

- Homework is often lost or never even understood, and schoolwork is incomplete or disorganized and experienced as overwhelming.

- Difficulty in producing written words means taking notes during a lecture is extremely difficult; this is increasingly problematic as courses become more advanced.

- Rigid, idiosyncratic thinking and slow processing time affect every aspect of functioning.

- Poor adaptation to novel situations leads to poor social and academic functioning, emotional shutdowns, and behavior problems.

- Difficulties with metaphor, analogy, humor, and reading between the lines cause poor comprehension and social alienation.

- Difficulty anticipating consequences and accurately understanding cause and effect makes the world a frightening and random-seeming place.

For the child with NLD or AD, the effect of deficits in information processing underlie all areas of difficulty, not just organization and academic learning. Social skills, pragmatic language, and even sensory-motor integration are all affected by information processing. Children with NLD or AD are likely to experience difficulties in any or all of the areas listed in appendix D. Program planning that includes interventions designed to take these deficits into consideration will be central to the success of these children.

# PART III

# What Now? Interventions and Program Planning

# 7

# Addressing Deficits in Organizational Skills and Information Processing

Earlier chapters described how, in NLD and AD, problems with social skills and visual-spatial and sensory integration and specific learning deficits all result, to some degree, from a disorder in information processing. Children with NLD or AD are likely to have above-average intelligence, but the ways in which information goes into the brain, is stored, and is eventually used are all "off." In this chapter, we'll explore how it's helpful to think of NLD and, to some degree, Asperger's disorder, as primarily disorders of information processing when we think about interventions and planning effective programs for these children.

Families are forever changed by these children. These changes can bring great joy along with inconvenience and hard work. It is very important that families of children with NLD or Asperger's understand and accept that the child will need accommodations from the rest of the family for many years.

# Information Processing Disorder

Ari's story, in chapter 2, illustrated how an information processing disorder can interfere with a bright child's ability to do her schoolwork. Although clearly able to take in information, Ari was unable, even with the help of her mother, to produce the report on Native American housing assigned by her teacher. The frustration both Ari and her mother experienced is not unique. Children with NLD or AD and their families often encounter the pain of feeling unable to do what others seem to accomplish easily, such as organizing separate pieces of information into a cohesive project, idea, or paper. The mention of upcoming projects is enough to make parents of these children cringe. The assignment all too often becomes one for the parent, as the child struggles to carry out tasks that may appear simple, but are mysterious and confusing to the child.

To learn, first we have to understand new information. Then we need some way of taking in the information and storing it in memory for later use. Chapter 6 used the analogy of well-organized dresser drawers to illustrate that how information is stored greatly affects our ability to retrieve it later. If underwear is sometimes put in the drawer with shirts, sometimes in the drawer with socks, and sometimes alone in its own drawer, it will be very difficult to find it. The same is true for information. Children with NLD or AD need help putting their information away in a useful fashion, so we must design programs that help them develop an organizational hierarchy of information.

It is difficult for these children to maintain organization of their schoolwork, home responsibilities, and basic day-to-day personal activities. Most of them do not readily adopt the methods of organization presented in traditional classrooms, which typically rely on visual information, such as the use of a binder with a list of daily assignments copied from the board. Organizing the binder itself, getting homework done and back to school, and completing notes or remembering to sign up for desired activities on time—all are expectations involving organization that the student with NLD or Asperger's cannot meet without direct intervention. The problem, as we have seen, is twofold:

1. The information is processed in an inconsistent manner and stored in memory in unusual and less-than-helpful ways.

2. The manner of retrieving information is poorly structured, and the child has to work extra hard to make the connections. This difficulty in retrieving information often results in frustration, and the child must extend extra effort just to maintain the will to continue to work.

Because these children have difficulty organizing information mentally, it should come as no surprise that they have trouble getting organized in the external environment, too. Therefore, this chapter will also address various ways to teach organizational techniques. And since stress can undermine any interventions aimed at helping the child with NLD or AD, we'll also take a look at sources of stress and interventions to help with this issue.

## Problems of Storage

First, let's take a look at specific issues associated with problems in storage of information into memory. Storing information involves transferring new information, or information presented in a novel manner, into memory. For children with NLD or AD, this can be problematic due to slow processing speed, missing the main idea, or focusing on the wrong details, all of which negatively impact how that information goes into memory. For each of these issues, we'll examine interventions that can be helpful—some in the classroom and some at home.

### Novel Information

The child or teen with NLD or AD can perceive practically all social situations and most academic experiences as novel. They have a limited ability to call upon previous experiences to help them in the current situation, and they can't process new information quickly enough to compensate for their lack of recall. But parents and teachers can help these children effectively deal with this deficit in their daily life by helping maintain routines and setting schedules.

## Intervention: Maintaining Routines and Setting Schedules

To reduce the child's sense that the world is novel, her daily routines should be consistent, clearly stated, and, when possible, posted on the refrigerator or some other central place. For children who don't read, parents can make a picture schedule. This is a series of pictures that shows the child (or another child) doing an activity; symbols may also be used to depict activities. The pictures can be drawings, photographs, or images cut out of magazines (for example, a drawing of a chair to remind the child to sit in the chair). At school, this series of pictures can be taped to the child's desk or to the inside of a binder, or it may be a flipbook that she carries with her. Another option is to post a picture schedule for the whole class on a bulletin board, making it accessible to all students and thus more normalizing for the class. The child with NLD or AD may need to carry an additional schedule, in pictures or in words, as she will be likely to forget to look at the posted schedule.

Posting a schedule at home also helps create predictability, even if there are changes for specific days of the week. The family of a child with NLD or AD needs to maintain a consistent and predictable schedule, and the concept of less is more is especially important for these kids. Scheduling some activities for these children is necessary, but overscheduling them or including them in the schedules or activities of other family members is difficult and often disruptive for the child. For example, it would not be a good idea to take the child with NLD or AD to her brother's soccer practice, then grocery shopping, then have her sit for an hour and wait for her sister at ballet. For many families, it may be a hardship to have to separate the schedules of the different children, and the concept may not be a good fit for families who prefer a spontaneous lifestyle or who have other pressing responsibilities. Yet without these accommodations, and without

```
┌─────────────────────────────────────────────────────────┐
│  1.  Wait in line                                       │
│                                                         │
│      ┌───────────────────────────────────────────┐      │
│      │  Picture of a student, maybe a Polaroid   │      │
│      │  of Ivan himself, correctly waiting in    │      │
│      │  front of the classroom                   │      │
│      └───────────────────────────────────────────┘      │
│                                                         │
└─────────────────────────────────────────────────────────┘
```

Figure 7.1    Ivan's School Schedule: A Sample Card

a willingness to adjust the family's activities, the child with NLD or AD is likely to suffer. Creating a daily schedule at home may seem like a lot of work, but it is time that pays off in less confusion and resistance and fewer meltdowns during the day.

## ■ Ivan's Story

*Ivan is in the first grade, and although he can read many words, his comprehension of what he has read is not strong. So although he can read instructions, he cannot necessarily follow them. The following schedule, using both words and pictures, was designed by his behaviorist for use at school; a separate one was designed for use at home.*

*Ivan's schedule is written on two series of five-by-eight-inch index cards, white for school and yellow for home. There is one card for each activity or time period Ivan needs to keep track of, and Ivan has the cards with him at all times in a handy and appealing decorated cover. The group of cards is ordered according to his day and is held together by a ring clasp. The order can be changed, activities can be added or removed, and new cards can be made to help prepare him for changes. When adding or removing a card, Ivan's teacher or one of his parents would explain the change and make sure Ivan saw it and understood. Ivan is likely ask about any change many times during the day.*

*Ivan's set of cards for school appears below; each would have a picture or symbol and a phrase, similar to the example in figure 7.1. If the same action is done at different points in the day, as with cards 1 and 9 below, the card should be the same, since the same behavior is expected. Explicit directions may be required for relatively unstructured time, such as recess or lunch, because children with NLD or Asperger's have more problems during times of social chaos and unpredictable interactions with peers than in a classroom with a teacher and structured tasks.*

1. Wait in line

2. Put lunch and coat away

3. Go to desk

4. Reading

5. Math

6. Put books away

7. Wait for recess

8. Recess (may require more than one card)

9. Wait in line (copy of card 1)

10. Go to the music area

11. Go to the story area

12. Lunch (many cards possible here)

13. Wait in line

14. Go to desk (copy of card 3)

15. Art or spelling (two cards; used on separate days)

16. Pack up books

17. Check desk

18. Wait for dismissal

```
1. Sit in the car with seat belt on

    ┌─────────────────────────────────────────────┐
    │                                             │
    │   Picture of a child, maybe Ivan himself,   │
    │   with a seat belt on                       │
    │                                             │
    └─────────────────────────────────────────────┘
```

**Figure 7.2    Ivan's Home Schedule: A Sample Card**

*For home, the concept is the same. Ivan's parents and behaviorist worked together to develop the after-school routine described by the following list of cards.*

1. Sit in the car with seat belt on

2. Put coat and backpack in room

3. Wash hands

4. Snack in kitchen

5. Homework for thirty minutes

6. Computer time for thirty minutes

7. Set table with sister

8. Dinner

9. Bath

10. Brush teeth

11. Reading with Mom or Dad

12. Lights out at 8:30 p.m. and time for sleep

## Intervention: Preorganizational Skills

If a schedule is to be an effective tool, the child with NLD or AD will need two sets of preorganizational skills (skills that are needed if a person is to benefit from organization techniques): knowing where to find the schedule and the ability to follow a schedule. These skills are actually more generalized and involve an ability to follow a set of expectations, whether a schedule, instructions to follow, or general social or behavioral guidelines. All of us follow rules or have to meet certain expectations, and all children need to learn to handle these expectations and follow the rules in different situations. For children with NLD or AD, it is very important that parents and teachers begin to train them in these skills at an early age and in differing ways for different settings, such as home, school, and community. The child will need to practice these often. Let's take a closer look at these two skills.

Although it may sound simple and obvious to know where to find a posted schedule (or instructions or other written expectations), the child with NLD or AD will have to be reminded to look on the board (or wherever) for the schedule of the day, and she will have to practice, looking for it over and over until she looks automatically. As these children mature, they will also need instruction and practice in skills like knowing to look for the Department of Motor Vehicles in the state government section of the phone book. Children with NLD or AD will also need practice following a schedule (or instructions or other written expectations). They will need to be taught to check off the steps as they go and to complete one thing before they start another.

Starting early is wise, because students with NLD or Asperger's will need both of these skills in upper grades. It is also much harder to get into the habit of following a schedule if you start later. Specific techniques for learning to follow a schedule will need to be developed for these children in many different settings: at home, at school, and in the community.

## Slow Processing Speed

Slow processing speed involves the inability to quic.. information to form an answer or behavioral response. Those with NLD or Asperger's suffer due to their slow processing speed in many situations—academic, social, and job-related—and throughout life. Though slow processing speed is clearly a problem at the brain level, to a certain degree this problem can be effectively dealt with if the person is willing to work to overcome the problem. Three major interventions can be helpful: openly discussing the issue, teaching focusing techniques, and teaching organizing techniques.

### Intervention: Discussing the Issue

As the child matures, openly discuss the problem of slow processing speed, or any other cognitive difficulties, for that matter. This intervention is central to all other interventions in this book. It is important to give these children the language and knowledge to understand what is happening to them. This doesn't mean you are granting the child permission to just accept the problem and not work to change or compensate. On the contrary, these children are empowered when they understand that they have strengths and weaknesses. Open discussion of your child's assets and deficits helps you support her strengths and help her take control of his or her weaknesses.

### Intervention: Teaching Focusing Techniques

For many of these children, their internal world interferes with their ability to focus on the activity at hand and is part of the reason they have a problem with processing speed. Clearing the clutter from their thinking (like clearing the clutter from their binders, their rooms, and their computers) is essential to many interventions that improve their organizational skills and information processing.

Learning to maintain focus allows the child with NLD or AD to address the ongoing issue of slow processing speed. Maintaining appropriate focus will take practice. Often, the first issue in learning to focus is learning to ignore or deal with novel situations, which increase stress. Stress, in turn, creates internal interference with the child's input and retrieval of information; it's almost like a distracting noise.

Breathing techniques to clear the mind and reduce stress have been very successful with these children and can be taught by many psychologists in a short intervention.

Self-talk, which can help the child ignore intrusive, interfering thoughts, may also prevent her from becoming overwhelmed. Here's an example: As the teacher gives instructions, the child becomes overwhelmed by the series of instructions because of her slow processing of the information. She starts to shut down and give up on the assignment. But by using self-talk, a skill taught by speech therapists or psychologists, she can focus and calm down. It is most effective when designed specifically for the needs of each child, but as an example, the child might learn to say to herself, "Take a breath, write the *number* of instructions only and a keyword for each, then go back and see what I remember for each number. I can do this, and if I get confused, I can ask the teacher to help me."

## Intervention: Teaching Organizing Techniques

As these children begin to understand their problems with processing information and improve their focusing skills, they can use techniques for organizing themselves to move beyond their processing limitations. With help, they can create a series of steps that keep them moving and develop a mnemonic to remember it. In the preceding example, the child might use CLWR:

- **C:** *Clear* my thoughts.

- **L:** *Listen* to the instructions but also *look* at my laptop (looking at the teacher may be distracting and slow her down).

- **W:** *Write* the number and a key word.

- **R:** *Return* to the list of numbers; *review* what to do.

The list of steps to stay on task and keep moving ahead can be on the desktop of the student's computer screen or on a card taped to her desk. For this approach to be effective, both the teacher and the parents must support the intervention. A word of caution: Keep in mind that one set of steps is enough; too many cards or mnemonics will get confusing.

In conversations, these children need to develop skills in making time to think so that they can organize their thoughts. This involves saying out loud what they are doing internally. Here's an example: If a teacher asks the child a question in class, the child is likely to take longer than average to answer. As a result, the teacher (and others) may think the child isn't listening or that she refuses to answer. She can remedy this by saying out loud something like "What is the plan for the school trip on Tuesday? Let me think ..." This lets the teacher (or whomever) know she heard the question and is thinking about it and also alerts them if she got the question. Alternatively, she might say something like "Please give me a minute to organize my answer."

If the child needs a more general way to stay focused and organized, the simplest intervention for her to use is externally controlled. The teacher or parent acts as the organizing agent, at least until the child develops more skills and can take over. The child is instructed to use a cue, like raising her hand in class, alerting the teacher to verbally or visually prompt the next step. Using cue cards with short statements or single words as prompts is a visual cue some kids prefer because they don't want to attract attention in class. The teacher can put the appropriate card on the child's desk without attracting much attention. For example, the teacher could have a set of laminated index cards on his desk that say things like "What's next?" or "Write something" or "Do you need help?" He can use them to prompt the student when he sees that she has drifted off or appears to have stopped working. Keep in mind that any interventions are unlikely to fix the problem completely; this issue will likely need to be addressed throughout the person's life.

## ■ Petunia's Story

*Petunia is fifteen years old and has been riding public transit for over a year now, having been taught by her mother how to get from home to her computer class on Saturdays. Things went very well until one Saturday when the bus was late and Petunia missed her transfer at the next stop. Although she and her mother had rehearsed what to do if this situation came up, it also happened that an altercation between two other people occurred while she was waiting. She became overwhelmed by the noise and shouting and got up to move away from the problem. As she was walking away, a bus came, and Petunia found herself confused over whether this was a bus she could take or not. The more she thought about it, the more confused she became, and she forgot to do what she had been taught: get on the bus and ask if it was going where she wanted to go. Instead, she sat immobilized for over twenty minutes until she calmed down enough to call her mother and get instructions about what to do.*

*Petunia has many skills and she eventually dealt with the situation, though her NLD clearly affected her functioning. Her mother had done the right thing by teaching her, over the course of many years, several ways to solve problems: Ask for information, sit down and calm down, and call home. Petunia is still likely to experience stress in unexpected situations throughout her life, but she has many tools for dealing with the situation, the most important being the knowledge that she can get help and solve the problem.*

## Getting the Main Idea

Without realizing we were learning it, most of us have developed an ability to understand the main idea of an assignment or a presentation—in other words, we get it. We may argue about details, but we understand the main point. This is not so for the child with NLD or AD. These children miss the main idea, so they often cannot see or remember the purpose of a lesson, reading assignment, or lecture without help.

Helping the child learn to identify the main idea is one of the most useful interventions a teacher or parent can initiate. Learning to identify the key idea and then remember that idea will help the child learn to link ideas, finally finding the connections between bits of information that have eluded her. Creative teachers develop practice activities for identifying the main idea. There are too many to describe here, and frankly, teaching how to identify the main idea is nothing new. What is new is getting across the need to do more of it for students with NLD or AD. This includes teaching and reviewing on this topic all the way through high school.

## Intervention: Getting the Main Idea at Home

At home, parents can review with the child what the main point of a TV program or storybook was. Help the child keep the ideas simple and learn to sum up the main idea in one or two sentences. This is not a play-by-play retelling of the story. It is learning to see the forest and ignore the trees.

For example, let's say Kevin watches his favorite Saturday morning cartoon with his father, who patiently sits through it with him. At the end of the program, his dad asks him, "What do you think this program was about, Kevin?" Kevin may start to retell the show in no particular order, just hitting on the action scenes or whatever caught his eye. His dad, who had been paying attention (and maybe even keeping a few notes for himself, as these characters are new to him), helps Kevin review the main idea of the show. "Well, these things are true, Kevin. But let's see, the main idea of the show was how Bobby didn't follow directions and got lost and his friends had to rescue him." Notice how Kevin's dad lets Kevin try to tell him what the show was about and acknowledges that his observations are true. The father also uses the term "main idea" to reinforce what he wants to hear.

This exercise opens up the possibility of discussing related ideas, uses language as a means of interacting, and teaches the concept of the main idea in a fun way. A word of caution is in order: Keep the "teaching" to a sentence or two, like Kevin's dad did. Long-winded discourses on the point of the TV show will lose the child as easily as the show did. Be patient with your child, and yourself; this is actually a very difficult task.

To really achieve success in teaching the main idea, begin early and reinforce the concept often. Many teachers will tell parents they already do this. No doubt this is true, and the reinforcement provided is enough for the average student. But for those with NLD or AD, the usual curriculum is unlikely to be enough; extra focus and practice will be needed.

## The Devil Is in the Details

Although understanding the main idea is crucial, focusing on details is also important in learning. Details add color and spice to ideas and concepts in many fields of knowledge, and they help many of us remember information. Unfortunately, children with NLD or AD tend to focus on details that aren't central to a concept but instead are unusual or unrelated. Furthermore, an inability to identify the main idea and a tendency to focus on the wrong details adds to the problems these children have with reading between the lines. This is clearly related to their overall information processing deficit. The child who listens to the story of Little Red Riding Hood and doesn't understand that the wolf has replaced Grandma and is trying to trick (and eat!) Red has missed the main idea. The child may have focused instead on the picnic lunch Red was carrying and then started thinking about what would be in the picnic basket, what she likes for lunch, and maybe what's for lunch today. This line of thinking has taken the child far afield from the story and in a direction quite different from that of most of her classmates.

Focusing on the wrong details affects these children in many ways. They are likely to miss details they need to know for assignments, and they often make mistakes in following the directions on a worksheet. When the class is following along reading from a textbook, the child with NLD or AD may be on the wrong page, unaware of what the problem is, and feeling confused because she doesn't understand what is going on.

## Intervention: Simple Instructions Clarify Which Details Are Important

In all situations (on worksheets and tests, and in verbal directions at home, at school, or elsewhere), the best interventions follow these guidelines:

- Directions are simple and clear.

- The fewer directions there are at a time, the better.

For example, give one or two directions, wait for those to be followed, and then give one or two more. Follow these concepts in all dealings with children with NLD or AD. Keep in mind their issues with processing speed, and never assume they know what you mean. Telling the child, "I don't want to see you eating candy in my class again!" may only succeed in getting her to eat in class when you are not looking. The child's literal or concrete understanding of that statement can lead her to feel the emphasis is on whether you see her eat. Eating when you're not looking is not an attempt to manipulate you or be a class clown.

Assuming the child knows how to do a task may actually interfere with her ability to follow the directions. For example, consider a student with AD who has a school chore to empty the classroom garbage cans and take the garbage to the large bin in back of the school. The teacher's assumption that the student knew how to do this effectively was incorrect. Although she clearly could take out garbage since she did it at home, at school, she transferred the skill from home exactly, that is, she took one bag at a time all the way to the back of the school. This resulted in ten trips to the bin, taking significantly longer than her teacher intended and making her late for her bus. It wasn't until her teacher discovered the problem and taught her to empty all the classroom bags into one large bag and then take that one to the bin that she was able to do the task effectively.

# Problems of Retrieval

The second area of organizational deficits is the breakdown that occurs when the child tries to retrieve information from memory and tries to integrate ideas and create a workable whole. The issue revolves around difficulty in creating an internal hierarchy of thinking—connecting thoughts to one another and assigning differing levels of importance to thoughts or ideas. This is not to say that children with NLD or AD cannot do this; the problem lies in their ability to acquire these skills fluidly and without help. Let's take a look at key problems in this area—difficulty reading between the lines and making connections; and problems with fluidity in the production of work—and interventions to help with these problems.

## *Metaphor, Analogy, and Reading Between the Lines*

Children with NLD or AD are concrete thinkers; they take things very literally. To them, words mean one thing, and one thing only. Obviously, this does not reflect reality, especially in a language like English, where words and phrases commonly have more than one meaning. For example, the phrase "put the card in your hand" has different meanings based on the context. If you were at an event where you need to hand a card to someone, you would put the card in your hand and hold it out. But if you were playing a card game, this phrase would mean to add the card to the cards in your "hand," meaning the group of cards you already have.

The use of double meanings of language has long been a source of humor, probably ever since humans have been able to speak. Children with NLD or AD have real trouble understanding such forms of humor. This is not because they are stupid, as they often feel, but because the source of this humor is not something they understand easily. The ability to "read between the lines," the subtle skill of understanding implied meanings, is similar. These children do not understand subtle or implied meanings, and this can lead to social embarrassment.

Their reliance on concrete thinking and literal interpretation of language affects their understanding of analogy and metaphor. Analogy (drawing a comparison or pointing out a resemblance between different things) is used often, both in literature and in everyday language. Teachers use analogy in lessons all the time, for example, comparing certain internal structures in a cell to an engine that powers the cell. In our culture, not understanding analogy makes for many moments of confusion and is likely to have a negative effect on learning.

Failure to understand metaphor creates similar problems. Metaphor is the use of language to describe one idea using another idea. Describing the organizational system of the brain as being a dresser with drawers for information storage is a metaphor. Many children with NLD or AD would not find this image helpful without an explanation. That explanation would need to convey the idea that the dresser with drawers is just a way to think about the brain, a way to imagine in understandable words what the brain may be doing (storing information like you store clothes).

### Intervention: Direct and Overt Practice

Throughout history, parents and other adults have taught moral ideas to children using fables and parables, which convey ideas through metaphor. The stories of the boy who cried wolf and the tortoise and the hare, for example, teach us lessons about human nature using metaphors. However, the child with NLD or AD may miss the point of these stories; the trees may become the focus, rather the forest (and that saying is, itself, another example of the use of metaphor).

The child who cannot figure out metaphor and analogy will feel left out, not part of a group of people who understand these uses of language. For that reason alone, it becomes important to teach directly what analogies and metaphors are, how to identify each, and, when possible, how to understand them. For those with NLD or AD, it may never be the case that use of metaphor or analogy comes naturally. That isn't necessary. What is essential is that these children learn to recognize and understand this form of communication and, hopefully, to decipher and even appreciate it in literature, in the classroom, and in conversation.

## Fluidity in the Production of Work

When you consider all of the deficits in organizational thinking these children have, it is no wonder that it is difficult for them to produce work. This is not, as some people may think, because they are lazy. It is because the production of work requires that you have an end product in mind—a sense of the whole, the goal. If you haven't gathered the various parts of the project together in your mind or on paper, if you have been operating as if bits of information are discrete and unrelated, using them to create a whole is a mystery. The deficits in processing and retrieval make the process slow, cumbersome, and far from fluid and seamless. The end result is a sense of being overwhelmed, withdrawal, and less work produced.

### Intervention: Refusing to Lower the Bar

The first rule in helping the child learn to develop a work ethic and increase her ability to produce work is to increase her stamina. These children often back away from tasks seen as new, hard, or long. To learn the skills they need to develop, tasks must be broken into manageable bits. Each bit must be taught and practiced, and the child must be held accountable for accomplishing appropriate goals. The expectation for work and time spent on independent work should increase each year—a ten-year-old should not be working independently on only three math problems a day if she was able to work at that level when she was eight years old. Certainly, the difficulty of schoolwork increases over the years and this must be taken into account, but like running a marathon, you never develop the ability to run the race if you only walk around the block and never try to do more.

## Managing Stress

For learning to occur, not only must the teaching be effective, but students also need to manage their stress. All of the suggestions and interventions in this book will be less effective if the child is overwhelmed by stress. Effectively managing stress requires many levels of intervention at home and at school. No matter what the particular effects of NLD or AD on any given child, she will have to deal with some aspect of her disorder almost constantly. In terms of stress management, time management, appropriate planning, taking action effectively, and all the many other aspects of executive function, small successes may be all the child or her parents experience for many years. Yet it is important to hold these children accountable for their work and their responsibilities. The line between infantilizing the child by doing too much for her and overwhelming her by not providing support is a fine one. But parents need to find and hold that line at each developmental level, or the child they love will never reach her true potential.

## Stress in Novel Situations

Children with NLD or Asperger's experience stress in novel situations—situations where they cannot predict what will happen next. Given that they rarely can predict what will happen in any situation except those they practice, this experience of stress is frequent. Imagine what it would be like to experience day-to-day interactions and everyday expectations as new. Remember learning to ride a bike or drive, or attending a new school? These experiences are novel to most people the first time they engage in them. Remember the anxiety, the high level of attention required, and the uncertainty over what to do next? All of these are a common and ongoing experience for children with NLD or AD, as they find most experiences novel. Developing stress management techniques that the child or adolescent can use anytime she feels stressed can help her overcome organizational deficits and use the skills she's been taught.

### Intervention: Classroom Setup

One way to reduce stress, especially for younger children, is to organize the classroom in a clear and uncluttered manner. Ideally, a work area should be designated—an area which should be separate from a reading area and from any other areas the class might have, such as spaces for science, play, or art. This way, students have an added cue about what sort of thing will happen in each area, even if the activity itself differs from day to day.

### Intervention: Setup at Home

At home, the same concept applies. These children need an area that is just for schoolwork, where supplies and materials can be stored. This does not have to be a separate room; it can be a desk with shelves or a set of stacking baskets for paper, folders, schoolbooks, and other supplies. There should be limited distractions nearby; for example, the space should not be in front of a window, which can be very distracting. There should also be easy access to adults; in other words, the child should not be off in an area where no one checks on her to make sure she is on task and getting work done.

### Intervention: Prewarning

Engaging in an interaction or being asked to meet an expectation, even in a familiar environment, can constitute a stressful novel situation for the child with NLD or AD. Whenever possible, the child should be prepared for the fact that new information is forthcoming, especially if that information will require a prompt answer. This technique, called prewarning, might sound something like this: "I want you to clear your mind and focus on what I am about to say. I am going to ask you a question I need an answer to...." This approach is also helpful if you want the child to perform a task, read out loud, or engage in an activity with others: "I will have Joan read, then Bobby, and then you, Sally. I will tap you on the shoulder to let you know your turn is coming. Everyone keep track of the reading as we go." Telling children with NLD or Asperger's what is about to happen is central to their success at meeting expectations. Telling them you will ask them to repeat back what you said also increases their immediate attention. Prewarning reduces the stress from novel situations by making the situation or activity more predictable, and it also helps the child clear her mind of any internal distraction that may be occurring.

Using physical proximity as part of the prewarning process can help; for example, moving closer to the child or placing a hand on her shoulder if she can tolerate touch. Other physical cues can also help the child stay focused: a hand signal, an object placed on her desk, a verbal reminder. For this strategy to be effective, the teacher and student must discuss it and agree upon it beforehand.

## Teaching Organization Techniques

For many parents of children with NLD or AD, it becomes second nature to organize their children. Many parents will say that, frankly, it's just easier to do it themselves. A word of caution is in order here. Teaching organizational skills by doing the organizing for the child has a place in the continuum of learning, but only as a form of modeling and a means of supporting the child in acquiring new skills. To continue to organize these children—to clean their rooms, keep their binders in order, write their assignments down and check them off—in short, to take on the actual work of organizing for them—can become a roadblock to learning to do these things for themselves. Strive to move from doing things for the child to doing things with the child to allowing the child to do things alone, even if this means that the child sometimes fails. Failure helps these children (and all of us) develop coping skills and a tolerance for frustration.

By high school, children with NLD or Asperger's need to have some strategies they understand and can use to deal with their disorder and the resulting organizational difficulties—unless, of course, their parents want them to remain at home with them forever, unable to function independently. Teaching organizational skills requires consistency, simple and clear expectations, and a realization that this is a complex problem that will need to be addressed in all aspects of the child's life.

## Intervention: Parental Role Models

It is important that you model the behavior you wish the child to emulate. In plain terms, this means that parents of children with NLD or Asperger's need to organize their own lives in addition to keeping the child's home environment and life organized. Although this may be difficult, a good organizational structure must be modeled and supported in the home environment if you are to have any hope of creating fundamental change for your child. Some parents may need to hire a coach to help them meet the demands of organizing themselves. Life coaches who specialize in organizational skills can be an affordable and valuable resource for parents.

## Computers and Technology

Technology can be a great asset in organization, and it will be discussed in greater depth in the next chapter. For now, consider technology a positive. Model its use and help the child see it as something that can be used to address a disability that affects her functioning. But keep in mind that although many children with NLD or Asperger's will report that they have excellent computer skills, for many of them their computers are, in fact, as disorganized as their own brains. Learning good organizational skills on the computer—using the file-saving systems, folder hierarchies, and various data management programs—can teach them ways of organizing their own thinking that they might not otherwise grasp. The computer can be a wonderful analogy for their own minds.

## Coding Systems

Coding systems can help the child with NLD or AD recognize patterns or reduce her confusion in managing paper and information. Systems of color coding (for example, using colors to denote various classes or chores) is often of only limited success. Color is not necessarily something of great interest for many children with NLD and therefore may not help them remember. Those with Asperger's may respond better to an organizational system that uses color. For example, if a teacher prints worksheets in certain colors for certain topics, a matching set of colored folders or colored binder tabs may help the child with AD keep things where they belong.

A numbering system, a system that uses words and numbers, or even a rhyming list or sayings that the child can remember may be more helpful. Auditory input is often more meaningful for these students, and a coding system that can be remembered through auditory triggers may be more successful. The use of a rhyme to remember a rule often works, not unlike the familiar "I before E, except after C." These little ditties stick in the mind and are easier to remember. Various handheld devices for making schedules and organizing information (especially the type that can feed information into a computer) may become very useful for these children, especially as the technology improves.

Teaching organization is a complicated process, and frankly, no perfect system exists. Currently, the best systems that can be offered to these children are those designed and implemented by knowledgeable adults (parents and teachers alike) who are responsive to the challenges these children face. Programs are being developed, and as time goes by more effective models will likely evolve. Most children with NLD or Asperger's will require training and support in organization for many years, and they will need consistent support in this from adults: a parent who operates as the child's case manager, a teacher with special training, or an aide in the classroom.

It is essential that these children not experience repeated failures at organization and that they aren't punished for this disability. Creating adults who are forever dependent on others is not the goal of intervention with these children. The goal should be that, by the end of high school, they are able to keep track of their own schedules, assignments, and commitments, and if they don't, they are able to handle the consequences. The goal is to help them develop techniques and to remember and keep track of the information they need to function in the world.

# 8

# Learning to Learn: Interventions for Successful Learning Experiences

The development and use of organizational skills is among the cognitive processes involved in executive function, the ability to plan and predict and to organize and use information. These skills are under the control of the frontal lobe, which oversees thinking, judging, learning, and social skills. Individuals with highly developed executive function are good at planning and organization. They read social cues and adapt readily to novel situations. They display flexibility and adaptability in their lives. The opposite is true for people with NLD or Asperger's: Rigid thinking and reliance on routines are usually the main ways they survive. For people with these disorders, it is hard to learn the skill of flexibility. As yet, there is no program designed specifically to reduce their rigidity and increase their flexibility in day-to-day situations. The best we can do is incorporate certain guidelines into program planning.

Deficits in executive function also impact the person's ability to plan and manage his time. This can affect social and academic endeavors and add to the internal sense of stress and confusion, and it doesn't bode well for work and career. Executive function deficits also impact the ability to multitask and use various study skills and techniques, such as note taking. Interventions must be developed to address these issues as they arise. Effective approaches include being sensitive to the child's learning modality, helping the child develop time management and study skills, and using technology to reduce the need for multitasking.

## Using Planned Exposure

Exposure to different activities and experiences should be planned so as not to overwhelm the child. But planned exposure does not imply controlling the child's environment to such a degree that he has no life experiences to draw on and no practice at being flexible. For some children, carefully chosen outside activities, such as clubs, camps, or activity classes, are a good way to start. These activities may be different than the child's accustomed school activities: for instance, there may be fewer accommodations or more demands. Take horseback riding, for example, which involves exposure to an animal, a new setting, and a new set of expectations and stimuli. Though the child may perceive animals as unpredictable, they usually follow a defined set of "behavior rules" specific to their species. This can make interactions with horses rewarding for the child with NLD or Asperger's, who can learn these new rules. Horseback riding can be rewarding for these children because it taps into their sense of routine but also adds to their ability to adapt. See appendix C for other ideas for activities that can expand the child's range of experiences.

## Planning for Increased Social Expectations

As children mature, they're subject to increasing expectations, which means they'll need more teaching about how to handle life situations. Social pressures in middle school and high school are much more complex than those in elementary school, and activities with age-mates bring with them demands for more sophisticated social skills. Teaching these social skills requires careful planning and thought, but it's an important undertaking; otherwise the child is likely to become isolated as he matures. Activity clubs that tap into the child's special interest are a good way to include him in a social setting with only limited unstructured time. A sport the child cannot do or a club that is full of free time to socialize would not be a good choice, as the child is not likely to be highly successful in these activities.

## Allowing Ample Time

Children with NLD or Asperger's are smart enough to figure out what might be a good plan in many situations; they just can't do it quickly, and many situations don't afford them the time they need. In such cases, it is important that the child has been taught coping strategies such as remaining calm, asking for help, or speaking up (for example, "I'm not too quick with words; give me a few minutes and I'll let you know."). Many of these children and teens develop their own idiosyncratic ways of stalling and coping in stressful situations, but few of these are usually functional in the long run.

### ■ Brian's Story

*Brian has significant difficulty in thinking on his feet, and he is often in the situation of explaining what he is doing. This is partly because he is sixteen and partly because, with NLD, he has a relatively self-centered worldview. He goes about doing whatever he thinks is right without thinking about all the implications of his actions. One morning after arriving at school, he discovered he didn't have any pencils with him. To get full credit for the day in his homeroom, students were required to arrive prepared, including having the supplies they would need. Knowing this requirement, Brian chose to go into the classroom and rummage around in the teacher's desk looking for a pencil to "borrow." When the teacher found him going through her desk and confronted him gently, he stammered and stalled: "Well, ... uh, uh ... I ... uh, uh ...," and never answered her.*

*As he struggled for words, filling the space with meaningless chatter, she finally got angry with him. At this point he was too upset to explain himself at all. He would have explained what he was doing (even though it was a poor solution to his problem), but he relied on an old stalling technique he learned early in life. Unfortunately, this technique rarely works for him: When he avoids answering a question, the other person either fills in the answer for him or becomes angry with him. In the situation with his teacher, if Brian had been able to take a calming breath, he might have been able to focus on a simple rule: Answer the question, and only the question, dealing with one idea at a time. He might have been able to start a dialogue in which he could explain his thinking, flawed though it may have been, leading to some sense of resolution with his teacher.*

## Predicting Outcomes

Practicing what would happen next is often part of a good pragmatic language program with a speech therapist. This technique involves watching an acted scene or reading about an event without an ending and predicting what would happen next. The child or group discusses various possibilities, in the process learning general concepts about what behavior is likely to occur. Predicting outcomes is a very valuable skill organizationally, academically, and socially. It helps facilitate organization, scheduling, and developing a repertoire of behaviors. Without this ability, not only do children feel ill prepared for general functioning, they also cannot react well to unpredictable events, nor do they learn from these experiences, as their anxiety prevents any learning from making it into meaningful memory.

## New Coping Strategies

For these children, reliance on rigid rules and routines is, in fact, a coping strategy. Life is unpredictable and confusing, and routines and rules make the child feel safe. For many children with NLD or

AD, routines develop into obsessions and compulsions, as discussed in chapter 3. In this case, the child should participate in individual or group therapy aimed at treating obsessive-compulsive disorder. This treatment can be an important ingredient in an overall program for the child with NLD or AD. But removing these methods of coping without helping the child develop more effective techniques is likely to create a great deal of stress, as he is then defenseless against the stress and sense of confusion that are likely to follow. It is important to work with the child to establish healthy and effective coping strategies.

## Maintaining Attention and Concentration

Almost every issue facing the child with NLD or Asperger's is made up of overlapping problems, and because of that, overlapping interventions are needed. Processing speed is affected by attention and concentration, and attention and concentration are limited by these children's slow processing speed—as the brain processes the information more slowly or less effectively, they often lose attention, becoming distracted and going off task. In some ways, it's a chicken-and-egg problem: Does the problem with processing speed cause the attention problems, or do the attention problems cause the slow processing? Whatever the case may be, problems with attention, concentration, and processing speed in turn affect a child's overall organizational skills.

Maintaining attention is a problem that requires direct intervention. Although medication may be recommended for this problem, bear in mind that not all children with NLD or Asperger's suffer ADD (attention-deficit disorder). Interventions that move beyond medication may be needed to address these issues, including the following:

- ■ Remove distractions and clutter. As a general rule, less is more for these children—less paper, fewer instructions, less visual clutter, less noise. Clearing the clutter also applies to clean and orderly work spaces. The work space should be a specific area that is away from visual and auditory stimulation like TV or video games. Classrooms with busy, visually overwhelming decorations and displays are not a good choice for these students. These concepts also apply to the child's work area at home.

■ Provide headphones with music to help the child focus during work time. In general, this helps children with NLD or AD focus on their work by making them less likely to be distracted by the ticking of a clock or another student chewing gum or tapping a pencil.

■ Seat children with NLD or Asperger's in the front of the classroom. As with other students with attention problems, this reduces their tendency to be distracted by other students or other things going on in the classroom.

■ Let them move. These children need permission to get up from their seats periodically. Some access to movement can actually help these students maintain attention.

As you can see, the need for a classroom that accommodates these children's needs is a strong one. See appendix B for a wish list describing the ideal classroom for a student with NLD or AD.

## Time Management Problems

Problems with managing all aspects of time are common for the child or teen with NLD or AD. These problems manifest in many ways, and they affect both the child and the family. The most prevalent issues with time these children have include the following:

■ They are often late, as they don't keep good track of time.

■ They tend to feel pressured by time constraints.

■ They misjudge time: how much is left, how long something will take, how long they or others have been talking.

## Keeping Track of Time

A simple intervention, and one that is often overlooked, is teaching the child to tell time and use a watch. This may sound obvious, but children with NLD or AD often have trouble learning to tell time and will need specific, patient, and repeated teaching on this topic. In our culture, there is a tendency to use digital clocks or watches, and because they display a number, the child can easily give the correct answer when asked what time it is. But there is no way to use the digital watch to teach the relative aspects of time, such as how long it is from 10:30 to 10:45. On a digital watch, this is just a series of numbers that appear on a screen. To help the child with NLD or Asperger's understand time, use a clock or watch with hands. The movement of the minute hand and second hand around the face of a clock or watch is a much better tool for teaching about the passage of time than digital numbers. As discussed in the next section, a watch with a timer will be useful for other interventions and is therefore preferable.

## Learning to Notice Time

Using a watch to notice time is an example of learning to look for the solution to a situation and learning to follow a plan (or schedule or expectation). The first step to mastering time is to notice it. To teach this skill, begin with two simple time assignments, each of which deals with a separate aspect of time. The first assignment involves activities you want the child to do at a certain time, such as "Your assignment today is to tell me when it is 5:00 p.m." or "Your job in class is to signal when it is time to switch to computer lab." A watch with a timer or alarm is often useful and helps remind the child to look at the watch.

The second assignment involves activities you want the child to do for a certain amount of time. Using a timer, preferably one with a large area that shows time passing in a separate color, is helpful. Practice having the child do things for shorter or longer time periods. Ask him to compare the differences in time by having him experience activities of differing time periods. Cooking can be a good activity to use (food is a good motivator), as can a stretching activity wherein the child holds a stretch for differing lengths of time (this has many benefits but is unlikely to be popular). Asking these children to estimate how long they have been riding in the car, eating dinner, or watching a TV show is a good way to help them internalize the sense of time passing. An hourglass with sand is another great visual for this concept.

## Time Management

For children with NLD or AD, executive function deficits affect their ability to plan and follow through with those plans. When you consider the added problems with time management, it's easy to see why these children have such great difficulty in planning workloads or balancing activities and responsibilities. Many a child with NLD or AD has been known to make errors in judging the length of time it will take to complete an assignment or activity. Being chronically late to class may be partly a result of these children's being "lost in space" and losing track of where they are, but it also may be due to their having no concept of how long it takes to get from one room to another and how long it takes to pack up a backpack. These children are not trying to avoid class, and they're not having fun by missing the start of a class—the opposite is more likely true, as entering a class late is embarrassing.

Even if arriving late goes on for weeks at a time, the child is likely to continue being late unless he receives clear, focused teaching about what is wrong (time management) and how to fix it (for example, a plan for packing a backpack and getting to class, complete with the route). Just telling the child he is in the wrong by being late will not fix the problem, and assuming it will indicates a lack of understanding of NLD and AD. For change to occur, the child will need a plan to address the problem. The plan will need to take into account whatever is causing the problem with getting to class on time, which could be many things. The plan must detail what the child needs to do to avoid the problem, and the child will need to practice the new routine repeatedly before any change can be expected.

The best solution for managing class work and other assignments is for the child to get assignments ahead of time and for parents to help the child plan the upcoming week or month. Daily assignments are most difficult and shouldn't be given to the student with NLD or Asperger's until high school. It will take practice and planning for these children to develop their time management skills enough so that they can handle six different classes with daily assignments in each. For some, this may never happen, and a different schedule will be required, such as block scheduling or classes coordinated to allow for limited homework assignments. (Block scheduling involves fewer, longer classes per day than a traditional schedule.) Clearly, these children will need support for many years.

## Learning Modalities and Styles

Most of us have a preferred learning modality, a way of taking in information that helps us remember the information better. The majority of people would describe themselves as visual learners, remembering what they see more than what they hear. In truth, all of us get information from what we see, hear, feel, and even smell all the time, and we hardly separate that information by source in our conscious thinking. But when it comes to what we remember, each of us has a modality of learning that works best.

### *The Auditory Modality*

Some people, including those with NLD or AD, learn more effectively through the auditory modality, most easily recalling information they hear. These learners benefit from oral presentations of material, oral practice and review, and even from assessment that is presented orally. This is not to say they don't benefit from other modalities. The visual modality and kinesthetic modality, or learning through body and motor activities, also make a significant contribution to their learning. Activities such as labs or skits are wonderful learning components, as they involve both visual and kinesthetic learning. However, the majority of students with NLD or AD utilize auditory information as a primary source of learning. As mentioned earlier, they appear to have a relative strength in auditory memory and auditory processing, and they tend to rely on this information over other channels of learning, such as visual or kinesthetic.

## Other Learning Styles

In addition to the learning that occurs through perceptual modalities (visual, auditory, kinesthetic), learning also occurs either sequentially (step-by-step learning) or simultaneously (whole-concept learning). Just as each of us has a preferred modality, we also have preferred styles—though, again, most learners take in information in both styles. Our preferred style impacts how we learn in various settings, which may be more or less appropriate to our needs.

Children with NLD or Asperger's are most likely sequential learners. The characteristics of these children's preferred learning style are as follows:

- Step-by-step learning. This includes simple numbered directions, with each step defined and each component explained in order.

- Logical explanations that include details. It isn't enough to simply tell a student with NLD or AD that the first step is to put his name on the top right-hand corner of the page because you want it there. You may need to explain that having the names there allows you to quickly skim through to see if everyone's papers are there. He will see this as a logical reason and be more likely to remember what to do. These children don't intend to be disrespectful; they simply need to understand why things are done so that they can learn the steps to complete the task.

■ Information presented as fact and figures. However, it's important to remember that the child with NLD or AD will not necessarily see the connections between these pieces of information.

Learning style encompasses many aspects beyond sequential versus simultaneous learning. For example, inferential learning is what we figure out for ourselves after a series of experiences or activities that illustrate a point, a rule, or a concept. Children with NLD or AD are unlikely to succeed with this type of learning. This is important for parents to know when considering kindergarten or preschool programs, as some programs are designed with the inferential style of learning in mind. Such preschools are unstructured, offering learning experiences rather than lessons and requiring the child to discover concepts without recourse to a planned program. These sorts of programs aren't helpful for the child with NLD or AD.

Though there are individual differences, as a whole, children with NLD or AD have certain tendencies in terms of learning style. Characteristics that affect their learning include the following:

■ They are perfectionistic.

■ They learn to read and spell phonetically.

■ They memorize rules for language, math, and other subjects.

■ They don't do well with inferential learning or problem-solving approaches to learning; they need guided and planned learning experiences.

■ They need structured, predictable, routine, learning environments.

■ They are part-to-whole learners; that is, they learn the parts of a concept in order to learn the whole concept. In this respect, the child with NLD or AD is the opposite of a simultaneous learner, who learns the whole to learn its parts.

## Planning a Program Around Learning Modality

It is important that parents and teachers understand the child's preferred learning modality and design a program that uses the child's learning strengths to support his educational progress. Even with a diagnosis of NLD or Asperger's, any individual child will not correspond 100 percent to the picture presented here. A good assessment is essential, and classroom activities and materials should reflect the information about the child's learning style and needs that results from this assessment. However, in general, most children with NLD or AD will learn new information best if it is presented in auditory or modified lecture format, as follows:

- Use lecture format in conjunction with technology support (discussed below) to eliminate the need for multitasking, for example, taking notes while listening.

- Present information in small segments, with review and summary after each segment.

- Intersperse the teaching monologue with attention-getting strategies and review tools.

- Use brief activities to make a point.

- Use question-and-answer moments to keep the student involved and continually summarizing the information that's been presented.

- Use visual examples (pictures, video clips, Internet sites) and physical activities (skits, labs) because no one learns by just one modality.

- As a review tool and to help students get through more advanced or detailed material, audio books are great for children with NLD or AD, particularly for literature and history courses. Audio books can greatly add to the child's learning experience and increase his enjoyment of literature.

## Textbooks and Worksheets

Students with NLD or Asperger's often find worksheets and textbooks visually confusing. In the past few years, textbook makers and school districts have chosen to move in the direction of materials that are increasingly visually complicated. For the average student, use of colors and pictures and separately boxed information may be interesting, and it is reported to actually help them learn. Not so for those with NLD or AD. In many cases, teachers may need to redo worksheets, copying them in black and white with the visually confusing areas covered. Some worksheets simply have too much on a page: A math sheet with thirty problems may be overwhelming for these children. Copying that sheet with every other row covered over, so that the new sheet has more white space and is less visually confusing, may be a great help. Note that it is not enough to just tell the child to "do every other problem," as is common in some schools. The worksheet itself needs to be presented in a less visually overwhelming manner. However, as the student matures, it is a good idea to limit this practice and to help him learn to accommodate to more visual clutter and a greater workload.

# Multitasking

Multitasking is clearly a product of our current culture. The ability to do more than one thing at a time is often viewed as a strength, and in some jobs, it's a requirement. But for students with NLD or AD, multitasking is overwhelming. Single-tasking (a fancy way of saying "just doing one thing at a time") is often enough to ask of them, as they struggle to follow through with plans and tasks even one at a time. As they grow older, the single most glaring example of their inability to multitask is an inability to take notes while listening to a lecture. To succeed in higher education, this skill is necessary, so if they don't learn to multitask in this manner or develop some alternative approach that fulfils the same function, they will be unable to access or benefit from more advanced subject matter and learning experiences.

## Technology to Assist with Multitasking

Advances in technology can be especially helpful for students who have difficulty multitasking. Their problems with taking notes while listening to lectures can be addressed with the use of special whiteboards that allow the notes the teacher writes on the board to be directly downloaded onto students' laptop computers. These whiteboards (sold under the names Softboard, Webster, and Smart Board, to name a few) make it possible for the student to listen to and focus on the teacher while the notes the teacher is putting on the board appear on the student's laptop screen. When the student studies, he can open the file of the notes for that particular lecture to review the material. There is no way to directly inject the information into these students' brains, so they still have to study (study skills will be addressed later in this chapter). But this technology makes the process of getting the information clearer and more appropriate for the needs of students with NLD or AD.

This modification requires that the school has the needed technology and that the student has his own laptop. Investment in this technology for classrooms has the potential to serve many students. In the long run, it is more cost-effective, and more empowering for students than having individual aides taking notes for each student who needs this assistance. Although having aides take notes is an often-used modification that has the advantage of personal contact, it has some disadvantages: The student can easily lose the notes, and the student is not in charge of his own learning and is dependent on another person. For some students, the aide is necessary for other reasons, primarily social and organizational, but for students aspiring to greater independence and to a future in the working world or higher academics, dependence on an aide is not ideal at the middle school or high school level.

A simpler modification that's accessible to anyone is to use a tape recorder. This is good for younger students, and it requires less technology. The child can use a small tape recorder to record lectures in classes and any notes to self. Notes to self are just what they sound like— messages the student or aide records to help the student remember certain things. In addition, teachers can make tapes for the student and his parents, explaining assignments or reminding them of things the student is working on. The child usually appreciates the personal aspect of having the teacher's voice at home. Taped information can also be very helpful to confused parents who are trying, with varying levels of success, to understand their child's version of what he needs to do. Speech therapists and clinical psychologists can also make recordings for the child to reinforce skills he is working on, such as relaxation skills, behavioral cues, and assignments for social interactions.

# Concept Formation and Problems in Learning

Students with NLD or AD find themselves learning large amounts of seemingly unrelated bits of information. Even on topics that interest them, their difficulties with organizational thinking and integrating information make for a limited repertoire of generalizable concepts. Left to their own devices, these students tend to find themselves forever unable to move beyond a series of facts. Self-directed projects and pattern learning can help with this.

## Self-Directed Projects

One of the most valuable learning experiences for students with NLD or AD is to develop their skills at self-directed projects. The use of student-defined projects as a central part of the learning experience is a focus of the program at the Orion Academy, a high school specializing in teaching students with NLD or Asperger's disorder. In Orion's Personal Projects program, students work with a mentor teacher to plan, organize, and carry out individual learning projects that are presented to the school community every six weeks. There are four different types of projects at Orion: exploratory, breadth, depth, and personal growth. Students must produce work in each area during the year. The program includes producing weekly logs, developing outlines, and learning information-gathering skills. The final step, producing a presentation, is as important as learning the information itself. For our students, the point to be made is that if you can't explain what you have learned to another person, the fact that you know it may be of little use to you. In addition, the requirement to present the material addresses these students' need to keep in mind their audience; they must focus on the perspective of another person.

The fact that the process of carrying out the project is more important than the content of the project creates an exciting learning environment for students. Furthermore, in this approach, parents don't become responsible for the work their children produce. Rather, the program requires students to learn how to learn: They must understand how to find information on a topic of personal interest, how to gather that information in an effective manner, and, most importantly, how to organize that information into a meaningful whole that others can benefit from. When they succeed in this endeavor, they are making progress that can help them keep learning throughout their lives.

## Pattern Learning

Students with NLD or AD tend to overly rely on learning patterns. This style of learning is often seen as a strength that the child relies on for development of skills, and teachers and parents have used this strength to help children be successful in sports, memorizing facts, and learning the routine for the day. Unfortunately, this strength can be problematic if the child relies solely on the pattern without learning underlying concepts or recognizing the overall point of an activity. Learning to serve a volleyball by practicing a pattern of motor skills may be very helpful for a child. But the fact that he doesn't understand the overall point of serving the ball in the game of volleyball is a disadvantage. He still wouldn't be ready to play with others if he is focused only on serving, the part of the game he has learned.

For another example, many students with NLD or AD have difficultly with math, especially fractions. Well-meaning teachers often teach these children the pattern of converting fractions to decimals to make adding, subtracting, multiplying, and dividing fractions easier. This method may be useful in the short run because there is less stress and students get the right answers. Yet they still have no idea what a fraction is; the concept eludes them. When they get to algebra and are confronted with equations that include numbers presented in fraction format, they don't know what to do. The pattern they learned gets in the way and has to be undone before learning can continue.

## Homework and Study Skills

For children with NLD or AD, organizational deficits profoundly impact their study skills and homework. Like students with other forms of executive function deficits, these children have difficulty successfully completing homework across the board. The problem arises not only in knowing what the homework is, but in getting the work and materials home, completing the work at home, and, once it's complete, successfully turning it back in to the teacher. In addition, when the homework is to study, the student with NLD or Asperger's is often unsure what studying entails and thus has much trouble following through.

### A Word About Homework in General

Homework is a subject just about everyone has had experience with. We all remember homework, and many parents get the chance to reexperience it with their kids. Yet, parents rarely understand why the child has homework or whether is it actually an effective teaching tool. Most people accept homework as a given but have no idea whether data and research support it as a meaningful part of the educational experience. That's really a problem, as completing homework affects every family, and for most kids with NLD or AD, homework has been an area of difficulty and stress for many years.

The research on homework has shown that, in general, less is more. In fact, findings reported by Cathy Vatterott (2003), an associate professor of education, have supported the idea that homework, at least as usually given, can have a detrimental effect. The study found that very few teachers are actually trained in how to design and assign homework and that what is given ends up with students frustrated in efforts to teach themselves rather than be taught by the teacher. In addition, homework often relies on parents or tutors to do the job that has not been accomplished in school. It's true that the demands on both students and teacher in the classroom have increased along with the expectations for teachers to cover required material in a specific timeline. This increased demand coupled with loss of teaching time for testing and practicing for testing has made it harder and harder to meet curriculum requirements. Unfortunately, homework is often used to compensate for insufficient classroom time to cover the curriculum. Yet increased homework is not a guarantee for improved grades. Although homework is often justified as a means to develop study skills, this benefit can be outweighed by useless assignments and loss of time for family activities, exercise, and the development of a balanced life. Cathy Vatterott explores some of the downsides of homework:

> There's something wrong when homework "entrenches privilege" (Kralovec and Buell 2000). Used improperly, homework disproportionately causes students who are academically or situationally challenged to fail. Academically challenged students, already mentally exhausted and frustrated from a long day at school, attempt to do homework without a teacher. Situationally challenged students including low-income students, ESL students, students with illiterate parents, and students whose parents work nights have little incentive to do homework (Vatterott 2003, 64).

At Orion, our experiences support the view presented above. We have found it to be of little use to send kids home to do work that they need direction to complete. Because of their educational needs, students with NLD or AD are unlikely to be successful in unsupervised work (as homework usually is) unless or until they have developed competency in independent work skills with the academic material or type of assignment. The development of a balanced life is a something these kids will find hard to do, and putting roadblocks in the way by overburdening them with homework seems counterproductive.

This is not say that homework is entirely useless. The data reviewed did find that high school students gained some benefit from homework, but only up to two hours an evening; beyond that, the benefit was lost. The ability to set aside some time and work independently on activities that are understood and within the student's scope of skills can have a positive effect on future productivity and on self-esteem. The goal here is one of seeking that balance—some work at home, which the student should be able to accomplish independently, but not so much work that it detracts from time at home and other important activities. This balance requires developing appropriate homework activities (like completing work from the school day—not adding new work) and developing study skills such as reviewing materials using a school-directed study guide. Students with NLD or AD should have gradually increasing independent responsibilities, and homework, used appropriately, can be one of them.

## Homework Support

Several interventions can help these students clear the organizational hurdles they face in getting their homework done and turned in:

- In general, a second set of books should be kept at home. This eliminates the need to transport them and makes for fewer things to be forgotten or lost.

- Homework should be assigned for the week, and special projects should be assigned as far ahead as possible.

- Projects should have review points throughout the process so that the entire project cannot be left to the last night.

- Homework should be listed on the Internet so students and parents can check to be sure it is all done. If that is not feasible, there should be a coordinated system set up between home and school, for example, a homework sheet where the student writes down the work for each week, the teacher signs it to verify it's correct, and parents initial it when the work is completed at home. This system is useful in early grades to teach the child the skill of keeping track of homework and to give parents a simple way to make sure homework is done.

- A laptop computer, if available, limits the amount of paper transferred from school to home and back—and potentially lost. Students can complete worksheets scanned into the computer and then either bring the work back to school in the computer itself or e-mail it to the teacher upon completion.

- For ongoing organizational issues, a privately hired coach is often helpful. These people are usually teachers who have developed a specialty in working with disorganized students. They work one-on-one with the child to develop organizational skills and coordinate with the school to develop a plan to make these skills work for the child. Often, what these children resist doing for a parent they will do for a coach, teacher, or other adult.

## Study Skills

Study skills are valuable and need to be taught directly and reinforced often. It is never too early for the child to start developing good study habits. The child with NLD or Asperger's will need to have studying explained and taught, just like other skills he needs to learn. Just because the child tells you he is studying doesn't mean it's safe to assume he has any idea what that means. Learning to study effectively requires that the child learn several specific skills:

- Paying attention to charts and diagrams in books: Teach the child how these can be used as shortcuts to understanding and remembering key points.

- Understanding the main idea of an assignment: If the child has difficulty identifying the main idea, teach him to ask for help, as this is the single most important way to improve information retrieval and develop organized thinking.

- Listing vocabulary words and other key words in readings: This facilitates later review by being quizzed by a parent or classmate.

- Preparing for discussions in advance: The child needs to remember that when a reading assignment is made, the teacher will likely have a discussion of the material. Teach the child to take time to review the reading and predict some possible discussion topics that the teacher might ask about.

These specific skills can be taught and fostered, and with them the ability to remember information learned while studying. Here are some ways to foster good study skills:

1. Plan a definite time for studying and stick to it. There are different ideas about when study time should be. The argument for having the child study immediately after school, before any playtime, is based on experiences with students who find it difficult to give up play or other free-time activities. For these children, the shift back to a work or study mentality is too difficult and the result is often a tantrum or poor work quality. However, right after school, other children cannot regroup and maintain the attention and concentration needed for homework without a break. The decision about when to schedule homework time should be based on the style and needs of the child. The important point is to

choose a time and stick to it, making studying and homework the only things that happen during this time.

2. Divide study time into segments of no more than thirty minutes and schedule five- to ten-minute breaks between segments. For elementary school students with NLD or Asperger's, studying one hour a night is plenty. By middle school, the student should be working toward increasing this to one and a half hours every few days, and by high school the student should be able to tolerate two hours of studying per day (with breaks, the study period as a whole lasts about two and a half hours). Keep in mind that the slow processing speed experienced by most of these children increases the time homework takes, and to succeed in high school (and eventually at college), they need to develop the stamina to keep working. Consider it like training for a marathon— the marathon of life. Students with NLD or Asperger's face greater academic challenges than most people do, and they need to develop the strength to handle this burden.

3. Find an appropriate place for the child to study and make this the only place to study. Keep in mind the guidelines described in chapter 7: visual distractions, clutter, noise, and traffic through the area should be minimized. The space should be used only for studying, so it should not be at the kitchen table or on the child's bed. A note about studying in bed: Many children with NLD or AD experience sleep difficulties. Perhaps as a result of this, they are likely to want to study in bed. This should be discouraged. Using an area intended for sleeping for studying can easily disrupt the development of good study habits, and it can also interfere with establishing good sleep patterns.

4. Set a stop time for homework sessions and stick to it. This helps the child know that there is an end. For younger children, if the work is not done at the end of the study time, have a plan with the child to complete it later that day (if

possible) or later that week. This is one reason why having assignments for the entire week helps: you can plan ahead.

5.  If it happens often that all of the homework cannot be completed within the week, speak to the teacher about the possibility of limiting homework for a period of time to allow the child to catch up. In some classes this won't be possible, and as the work piles up, it creates anxiety for the child. At this point, you may need to discuss homework modification with the child's teacher. One way to modify homework is to have the child do only even-numbered problems or find some other way of reducing the volume of work while keeping the same concepts. As these children mature, this is less acceptable because they miss material, feel inadequate in relation to their peers, and don't progress in their ability to tolerate increasing workloads.

6.  Keep study segments the same on each study day. For example, a fourth-grader may have an hour and ten minutes set aside each day to complete his homework. The first twenty minutes is devoted to math, then there is a break of five minutes for a drink and conversation with Mom, then twenty minutes for reading and vocabulary assignments, then a break, and then a final twenty minutes for writing assignments. Each day this routine is maintained, with the final twenty minutes being the segment that depends on the weekly assignments, which vary. Set a goal for each segment of study time. For example, the goal may be to complete ten math problems or to read to a certain page in a book, or it may simply be studying.

7.  Take care of the logistics. To do a homework assignment, the child needs to know what the assignment is before leaving school so that he'll have the needed materials. Use the support ideas mentioned earlier—a second set of books at home and a way to be sure assignments get home—to achieve this aspect of good study skills.

## Staying on Task

It is important that adults supporting students with NLD or Asperger's remember the issues specific to these disorders. The tendency these children have to be distracted is real. Help them by using interventions such as providing a quiet place to study or headphones to lessen auditory distractions. These students may not be attentive to detail or may cling to the wrong detail; this is a serious problem. It means they will need to review their work with a parent, classmate, or mentor to be sure they have in fact done what was asked. Spell-checkers and other technological aids can be valuable for students with NLD or Asperger's, although many ignore these aids. On the other hand, always remember that making mistakes is part of learning, not just part of these disorders.

By high school, academic and social demands on these children will have increased to the degree that even students with high IQs are likely to experience difficulty. The trouble they have with multiple and complex directions can be lessened by requesting that instructions be simplified and assignments broken down into more manageable segments. Keeping a simple system of organization that allows the child to put papers and work in one place becomes even more important in the upper grades. Since staying on task during study time is also likely to be difficult, use multiple methods: timers, pictures, or flashcards. Using self-quiz methods, asking others for help, and writing notes to themselves can all help these students develop the study skills needed for upper-level work. All of these techniques make information retrieval less confusing. There are a number of excellent websites and books on developing study skills and more efficient time management tools. As the student with NLD or AD progresses to more complicated academic settings, these resources may be helpful.

## Teaching Considerations

To most effectively teach students with NLD or AD, it is important for teachers to have an understanding of specific problems that affect how these children learn—or fail to learn. With sensitivity to these problems, teachers can create an environment and lessons that enhance the likelihood that these children will succeed in learning. As we saw in chapter 6, NLD and Asperger's disorder both involve failures in the executive function. The deficits that are most often seen are as follows:

■ Difficulty in planning

■ Poor self-monitoring (keeping track of one's own actions and the effects they have)

■ Expression of incorrect, impulsive responses

■ Rigid behavior and thinking patterns

■ Failure to solve problems or search for answers in a planned and organized manner

■ Difficulty knowing when ideas or concepts belong together (for example, that math has different ideas and is different work from reading, though reading is often part of completing math homework)

With these deficits in mind, here is a brief list of points to remember when developing an academic program for children with NLD or AD. An excellent source of further information for teachers is *Asperger Syndrome: A Practical Guide for Teachers* (Cumine, Leach, and Stevenson 1998). Although the following list is hardly comprehensive, it provides a good starting place for both teachers and parents:

■ Always remember that NLD and AD are neurobiological disorders and that dealing with the surface behavior will not necessarily correct underlying deficits. These children will always have these disorders; what changes is the way they learn to handle them.

■ In these children, ability to use language does not represent ability to communicate, which is often significantly lower than their language level. Know the communication level of the child; that is, his ability to use language to interact.

- The academic program must include basic social skills. These skills include listening, not interrupting, taking turns, sharing, waiting in proximity to others (such as in lines), and working with others. Learning these skills will take time.

- The child with NLD or AD needs to learn how to behave socially, and this learning is often stressful and time-consuming. Academic learning may need to be seen as secondary for some children as they learn to function socially.

- A good teaching plan will include specific goals for developing skills in processing information. This plan will take into account the slow processing speed of these children and their need to be taught systems of organization.

- Be explicit and concrete in giving directions. Do not assume the child knows what you mean in a particular situation. For example, telling a child with AD to draw a card in a card game and "put that card in your hand" will not necessarily get that child to put the card with the other cards he is holding. Instead, the child is likely to simply hold the card in his other hand.

- Children with NLD or AD can easily become overstimulated and overwhelmed by auditory, tactile, or visual stimuli. This will impact what their classroom environment should be like, as well as the format of lessons and worksheets.

- Check to ensure that the child is attending to the main topic or activity of the moment. Don't assume the child is focused on the correct topic just because he is on the correct page in a textbook.

- Alert the child to his role in various situations or tasks, making your description of that role concrete and explicit. This will be especially important in social situations where the child may tend to feel like a victim, not seeing his own part in the interaction.

- Draw the child's attention to the use of gesture, facial expression, eye direction, and proximity in social situations. Develop cues to help him notice the things he needs to be aware of to understand the meaning of an interaction. A cue is a prearranged gesture (for example, a gentle touch on the arm to remind the child to focus on the speaker's face).

- The concept of pretending is neither natural nor pleasurable for these children; keep this in mind when designing activities for them.

- Homework should be appropriate to the child's level and modified to increase his likelihood of success. A system of communication between home and school is essential, and the use of supportive technology is highly recommended.

- These children often develop "expert status" on a topic of interest. Keep in mind that overfocusing on a special topic may be comforting to the child. Allow the child to utilize this competency with his peers and with you, but introduce ways to broaden his focus.

Several specific techniques can be especially helpful when teaching these children. Teachers should incorporate the following points into the curriculum for students with NLD or AD and keep them in mind in all program development:

- Make the beginning and end points of assignments and other tasks explicit.

- Use checklists or a numbered series of prompt cards with pictures, diagrams, or scripts to help the child complete a task, including the task of getting through the school day.

- Provide a model of the final goal or end product. This can be a verbal description or, for the child with AD, a picture.

- Ask the child to repeat back to you what it is you want him to do, including the goal. Be sure the child understands what the goal is.

- Be clear, concrete, and explicit in directions and expectations, and avoid giving too many instructions at once.

- Design programs to explicitly teach ways for the child to connect knowledge from one area to another, providing opportunities for him to generalize what he has learned.

- For the AD student, teach using sequences of visual cues; picture cards are one example.

- Focus directly on cause and effect, motives, and plot. These children are unlikely to see these connections without explicit teaching.

- When teaching social skills, offer the child explicit ideas on things he can do to navigate social situations. Help set up situations where the child can experience social success.

- Ideas and techniques used in occupational therapy can be very helpful.

- These children's arousal states are usually poorly managed, which interferes with their learning (the next chapter will provide more information on arousal states). A team approach with an occupational therapist, a professional trained to work with sensory and motor skills, can be invaluable in this area.

# 9

# Bodies in Motion: Addressing Deficits in Visual-Spatial Processing and Sensory-Motor Integration

In many cases, children with NLD or AD were unique even as infants and toddlers. For parents, this child was the "good" baby: easy to entertain, not constantly into things, self-focused, and self-comforting. On the other hand, some children with NLD or AD were inconsolable at times during infancy, seemingly overwhelmed by internal discomfort and described as colicky by pediatricians and well-meaning grandmothers. Yet as a group, even this latter group of children tend to be content when read to or talked to, and as toddlers they often prefer quiet activities to wild and rambunctious games. Their reliance on using language to explore the world—asking "What's that?" instead of getting up and grabbing the object to feel and then perhaps eat—is possibly the first sign of their limited use of sensory-motor (physical) behaviors.

# Sensory Overload

In normal development, children go through phases, often shifting between physical growth, language growth, and motor skill growth. Although there are no studies to date to support this idea, it seems logical that children with NLD or AD would find language and words much more comfortable than physical activities, so their development in the area of language skills would be self-reinforced; because language is more enjoyable for them, it is returned to more often. It seems that the child comes wired with a predisposition for difficulty with sensory information. These children are more likely to have problems with being overly sensitive to sounds and tactile sensations and their sense of smell and taste is often highly sensitive and idiosyncratic.

## Tactile Sensitivity

The feelings of tags in clothing, the cloth of long-sleeved shirts, or air blowing on exposed skin can be annoying to the point of distraction for some of these children. Bathing in general and shampoo in particular—the "lightness" of the shampoo on the head—can be unpleasant for them. People standing close, perhaps in hallways at school or when waiting in line, or the touch of a well-meaning teacher's hand on the child's shoulder are also potentially unpleasant experiences for these children.

This acute tactile sensitivity can affect day-to-day functioning. For most of us, the relative roughness or smoothness of fabric or furniture, or the proximity of other people is noticeable, but it hardly interrupts our use of objects or our concentration on other things. But for the child with NLD or AD, the way things feel, the tactile sensations, are often enough to trigger a full-fledged meltdown. It is important to note that these meltdowns are not tantrums in the sense that a spoiled child has tantrums. They are more likely to indicate that sensory overload has occurred and the child's processing system is shutting down. The child has reached a point of being unable to handle the stimulation she is experiencing, whether it's the texture of her clothing, the feel of a shampoo, or the closeness of another person. The explosion is the result of the overload.

## Auditory Sensitivity

A heightened awareness of sounds often creates problems for children with NLD or AD. Sounds that are loud (or too loud for these children) or repetitive, such as the ticking of a clock or a classmate tapping a pencil or chewing gum, are grating and annoying to the point of being painful.

### ■ Jamie's Story

*Jamie was eight years old when she began to notice that certain sounds in the classroom were impossible to tune out. She had been schooled at home up to that point and had never experienced a classroom full of students before. The ticking of the clock took her attention away from the teacher, and in her opinion, the school announcement system in her class was way too loud; she had to cover her ears whenever the principal addressed the school. Classmates tapping pencils while they were working annoyed her so much that she had to ask the teacher to intervene.*

*But all of these annoyances were nothing compared to the feeling inside her when people were chewing gum. The snapping and chomping was like fingernails on a chalkboard to her. She couldn't stand it. The only time she received a suspension from school was the day she leapt from her seat and grabbed a classmate by the arm, yelling, "Stop that. Stop that!" Her classmate landed on the floor, and Jamie was seen as the aggressor (which, technically, she was), all because this classmate was chewing gum in class. The teacher hadn't even noticed it, and the student himself couldn't have imagined that chewing gum could possibly be such a problem. Jamie wasn't proud of what she did and the other students began to see her as a little weird after that, but, in her view, what else could she have done?*

## Sensitivity to Smell and Taste

Parents of children with NLD or AD often report that their child has unusual food preferences long after the toddler years. Similarly, these children tend to comment on how something smells—often when others don't even detect the smell. It is interesting to note, though, that these same children usually don't notice when they themselves smell—which they often do because, as a group, they tend to resist bathing and changing clothes. Although these sensitivities have not been studied formally, anecdotal reports are frequent and suggest that sensitivities to smell and taste may be as much a part of these disorders as those noted for the senses of hearing, touch, and sight (these children can also be overwhelmed by too much visual stimulation, as discussed in chapter 8). The poor grooming that is so common among these children may arise from the fact that their sensory skills are askew, though it may also reflect their failure to notice that others notice them. (This second issue is one of social perspective and will be discussed in chapter 10.)

The unusual or limited food preferences these children have are all too familiar to their parents. Although these preferences are highly individual, anecdotal information suggests a general preference for bland, pale, nontextured foods, especially "white foods," such as saltine crackers, bread, cream cheese, pasta, and milk. Carbonated drinks seem to trigger mixed reactions, with some children finding the bubbles unpleasant and preferring juice or milk. This preference seems to be a part of the sensory wiring these children come with. In terms of intervention, it usually works best to offer these children more choices over the years, as their palates mature. It is not useful to get into a battle over food. Provide several healthy choices, including some "white food" if that is the child's preference. Set a good example with the food the rest of the family eats and refrain from offering poor choices like fast food or sweets. These kids have enough going against them without adding poor nutrition to the mix.

## Sensory Integration Techniques

For the child with NLD or AD, experiences of sensory sensitivity are real, and they affect the child's ability to attend, to concentrate, and to learn. The behaviors these sensitivities elicit can have a negative impact on the child's social relationships and sense of self-esteem. It is essential, then, that sensory integration training be a part of any intervention these children are offered, from an early age through high school.

### Modulating Arousal States

The first intervention a child diagnosed with either NLD or AD needs is a complete assessment by a qualified occupational therapist. This is because no two children are exactly the same. This assessment will detail the work that most needs to be done with a child, and from the assessment, a program that is tailored to the child can be developed. Certain programs, such as the Alert Program created by Mary Sue Williams and Sherry Shellenberger (1994), which most occupational therapists are trained in, have been very useful for children with NLD or AD. These programs help children learn to modulate their arousal states, allowing them to take in sensory information much more effectively. Arousal state refers to the level of attention and concentration a person has at any given time. Low attention, or a low arousal state, is to be droopy, drowsy, and easily distracted. High arousal is to be in an agitated, hyperalert state that makes a person just as prone to distraction as low arousal. Without an ability to modulate her arousal state, the child swings between high and low and is more likely to experience a meltdown. Using techniques to maintain attention and concentration without sensory overload, the child learns to avoid meltdowns and gradually develop ever-greater coping skills.

## Using Music

A portable music system with headphones is a very successful intervention for many children with NLD or AD. The music is predictable, so the child's attention remains on the work in front of her. Clearly, this intervention is not appropriate for group activities or direct teaching time. When using this intervention, it is important that parents and teachers keep track of when the child is choosing to listen to music. There is a fine line between using music to maintain focus and screen out distractions and using it as a way to avoid social contact with others. The latter is not an option to be supported, and if it becomes a problem, the intervention would have to be reevaluated.

# Inertia

There is a law in physics that says, in part, that a body in motion will stay in motion unless that motion is interfered with. In the case of children with NLD or AD, not only does initiating movement not come easily, but keeping the body in motion does not seem to be the law that prevails. Instead, as previously discussed, the child is likely to find herself poorly suited to both large and small motor activities, especially activities that involve visual-spatial skills.

## Teaching Fine Motor Skills

Tying shoelaces is often difficult for children with NLD or AD. This task requires fine motor skills (fingers moving the shoelaces) and visual-spatial understanding. In some ways it is like braiding: Learning to braid is easy for some people, who just get it, and close to impossible for others. In regard to tying shoelaces (or tying in general), don't start teaching this skill too early. Wait for the child's motor skills to mature to increase her chances of success, and use Velcro shoes until then. Just because your cousin Sally's daughter can tie her shoes when she's four years old doesn't mean your child needs to be able to do it at four.

When teaching shoe tying, or any motor activity for that matter, design a script—a set of verbal directions that help the child remember the pattern of the activity. Using language to support the motor skill is more likely to help the child succeed. Also, provide a model of what the finished product should look like: either an already tied shoe or a picture of one.

## Teaching Balance

Riding a bike or scooter and other similar activities require balance, and balance involves using multiple motor skills simultaneously. Such coordination is difficult for the child with NLD or AD. Again, wait to teach this skill. You're not in a race to see which child learns the most activities first. Learning balance first on a balance beam in occupational therapy or in an adaptive physical education class can add to the child's success. With patience and practice, the child can learn to ride a bike and do other activities that involve balance. For these children, it is especially important that safety be part of the teaching, and use of protective gear is a must.

## Teaching Direction and Orientation

As previously mentioned, children with NLD or AD tend to get lost more than other children do. This is a result of a couple of things: First, their brains don't register visual-spatial information the way the average person's does. And second, as a group, these children tend to rush along, especially in situations that are unknown. When traveling along a path, most of us notice (to some degree) the way we came, and we are likely to be able to retrace that path. We use our memory of what we saw, heard, or smelled and our sense of the spatial relationships between things to help us remember how we got from one place to another. The child with NLD or AD does not have this innate ability. She will need cues, verbal directions, and other specific help in remembering what to do.

At school, these children may need written directions or maps to help them learn the way from one place to another, for example, from the classroom to the cafeteria or bathroom. For some of them, maps will be less useful but counting the number of doors between the classroom and the bathroom will help. Point out landmarks, such as the big tree in front of the office or the blue water fountain next to the science room. In addition, the child should practice noticing the route and remembering cues with a supportive person (only use a peer if that child is able to help the child with NLD or AD with these cues). Cues might be landmarks (turn right at the water fountain) or small pieces of colored tape placed along the way to guide the child. Use colored tape only for younger students, and train them to eventually use landmarks and verbal directions.

In public places that are novel, use of a walkie-talkie can help the child stay connected to an adult if the child wants to try to be more independent. This is a useful activity to help the child gain confidence in new settings, like the mall or when using public transportation. The parent or other adult trails at a distance and the child (with a peer, perhaps) practices getting herself from one place to another. This activity increases the child's experiences of success and reduces the sense of helplessness she may feel in new settings.

# Dysgraphia

Dysgraphia, or difficulty in producing written words and letters, is a common disorder among children with NLD or AD. Even children with AD who are good at drawing often have difficulty writing letters and words, or writing words on command. Writing is not the same activity as drawing, and just because a child can draw does not mean she will be able to write well or fluently. For some students, the writing itself—the formation of letters—is adequate, but the process is slow and laborious. The effort required makes the act of writing unpleasant, and thus the child begins to avoid writing.

Many children with NLD or AD will also display significant discrepancies between their knowledge about a subject and their ability to write about the subject. Part of the problem lies in executive function deficits, but part of the problem is in the mechanics of writing letters and words. Writing is a visual-spatial task involving fine motor skills, and because of that, it is very difficult for many students with NLD or AD.

## Handwriting versus Keyboarding

As a rule of thumb, early on the focus should be on mastering handwriting: printed and cursive writing should be undertaken, as with all students, beginning in kindergarten and progressing through the third grade. Cursive writing may be easier for these children as the spacing of letters is less of an issue, but the production of letters usually remains a problem. It is important for the teacher to evaluate the particular problems the child is experiencing. Desk height, the fit of the chair, and the posture of the student all contribute to success in writing in particular and in learning in general.

At a certain point, usually sometime during the third grade, the child with NLD or AD becomes bogged down with the act of writing and her learning suffers. At this point, it is a good idea to introduce the child to keyboarding, using either an AlphaSmart (a word processor that looks like a small laptop computer) or a laptop computer. Teaching these students how to use a word processing program can alleviate the feeling of failure that writing manually creates for them. However, the AlphaSmart is only useful for younger students; it soon becomes more harmful than helpful because the small screen allows the student to see only a line at a time as it is typed and goes by. Although she can review what she has written before printing it out, the child can't see larger chunks of the document and thus may lose her sense of what she's written as a whole. For many school districts, AlphaSmarts are seen as an inexpensive, economical alternative when they don't have access to laptops for all children or if they prefer not to offer laptops to younger elementary school students. Although those decisions may make sense for school districts, they may shortchange the student with NLD or AD. Once these students are able to handle a laptop they should be given one, as this will make creating written documents and organizing their materials and notes in all classes a much more effective activity.

A computer has another advantage over the AlphaSmart: In addition to providing a sense of the document as a whole and its organization, a computer allows for transfer of information. Students may eventually need to have their worksheets scanned into their laptops so they can work directly on the computer to complete assignments in math or other subjects. Software exists to facilitate this. This approach also requires faculty and administrators who have access to these products and are able and willing to use them. These simple accommodations can make a huge difference for students with NLD or AD, allowing them to keep up with the work in regular education classes.

## Other Interventions for Physical Problems

Comfortable work positions and body posture are unique to each individual. In our cars we set the seat to suit us; in our homes we have a favorite chair or pillow. In classrooms across the country, desks are uniform and all students are expected to work in the same manner—sitting for long periods of time at these uniform desks. Most students are able to comply with this requirement, sitting and working as directed. But for children with NLD or AD, the desks and seats provided may actually hinder their ability to work and concentrate.

### Help for Poor Posture

For reasons unknown at this point, many of these children have poor posture and poor muscle tone. Poor muscle tone requires specialized remediation, which will be discussed below. Clearly, poor posture can result from the child's poor muscle tone, but it also seems to result from the way the child uses (or fails to use) environmental supports.

A chair suited to the child and a desk of the right height can make a huge difference. If there is any question about the suitability of furniture, the child's occupational therapist can evaluate it and make recommendations. In addition, children with NLD or AD often work better if they are allowed to stand at their desk, to pace while reading, or even to lie on the floor or in a bean bag–type chair. These accommodations, along with rules for the child to follow, can be made in an elementary classroom without much disruption of the class. Use of special seating (T-stools for example, which are seats balanced on a single leg that the child must balance on) may be recommended by the occupational therapist and can be a great help for the child in maintaining posture, attention, and production of work.

Children with NLD or AD often have a unique way of walking, as though they are carrying a great weight that causes them to hunch over, almost folding in on themselves. This posture conveys insecurity to less-than-well-meaning peers and is often referred to as the "kick me" walk. Many of these children will either sit in a similar hunched-over manner or lean back in their chairs, rocking the front feet of the chair off the ground and attempting to balance precariously on the rear legs. Because their poor posture can eventually create real spinal problems, it should be corrected as soon as it is noticed.

## Help for Poor Muscle Tone

For children with NLD or AD, poor muscle tone seems to be a self-reinforcing problem: Because of poor muscle tone, the child finds sports harder or less pleasant than other solitary activities, so she avoids them, and thus her muscles are not pushed and don't develop. As time goes by, the child's peers become stronger and more accomplished at physical activities; feeling uncomfortable and uncoordinated, the child with NLD or AD falls further behind and is even less likely to want to try. Ultimately, this affects posture, stamina, and general physical health. Establishing a program to develop the child's physical skills is as important as nurturing her mental skills, for without posture, stamina, and muscle tone, learning will be compromised, too.

The physical program should be developed by someone knowledgeable about proper form and the appropriateness of various activities for different age levels. For example, formal weight training needs to be taught by a trained professional and should not begin before the child is fourteen years old. However, there are many weight-bearing activities that build both muscles and flexibility and can be taught at an early age. Carrying groceries in from the car, vacuuming, and digging with a shovel all help build muscle control and flexibility and also include the child in activities that are part of daily life.

Physical training programs for children should include the following components:

- Warm-up activities

- Flexibility and stretching exercises

- Aerobic activities, with slow and steady increases in the amount of time the aerobic activity is sustained

- Skills training for games and sports the child is likely to participate in, such as kickball, basketball, and softball

Once the program is in place, a high school student or personal trainer might be found to serve as the child's coach.

Visual-spatial and sensory integration interventions are a necessary part of any program for children with NLD or AD. Often, well-meaning professionals assume that these interventions are only valuable for young children, and so services or programs end when the child enters middle school. This is unfortunate, as the use of a trainer, modified Alert Program techniques, or classroom accommodations for posture and dysgraphia are often needed all the way through high school. Parents must advocate for their children and make services in this area as much a priority as academic services.

# 10

# Social Competency: Issues of the Self, Others, and Self-Esteem

The Books

*I read of fantasy*
*Of dragons and knights,*
*Goblins and ghosts.*
*I read of science*
*With ships in space and guns.*
*I read of mystery,*
*Of murder and deceit,*
*Of trickery and lies.*
*I read of many things*
*Why can't I read your eyes?*

—Lawrence Hsu, age fifteen
(*Sacred Grounds Anthology*, 2001)

Throughout this book we have looked at NLD and Asperger's disorder as disorders that have in common a deficit in the manner in which the individual takes in information and uses that information—an information processing deficit. It seems like a small thing, processing information. It is something we all do every minute of every day. But because we do it every minute of every day, it is hardly a small thing. The ability to successfully process information is central to an individual's ability to function in just about every aspect of life. It is critical to the ability to learn, to function in the world, and to be successful socially.

In this chapter, we'll explore the effects of information processing deficits on social competency among children with NLD or AD. Incorrectly judging the mood or emotion of someone else; not reading that your comments are boring or inappropriate; standing too close to others; avoiding responding to others because of sensory overload from information coming in: all of these issues result from an information processing deficit and have negative effects on these children's social success and, eventually, on their self-esteem.

## ■ Rachael's Story

*Rachael, now sixteen years old, is a slim brunette with NLD who has a loving nature and a naive acceptance about her. She is often disheveled looking; even though her mother takes great pains to buy her the latest "cool" clothes, Rachael never can remain looking put together. Rachael tells of her experiences in middle school and her first year of high school, where other children teased her for being messy and unkempt looking, for being weird and naive, for simply being herself. She didn't shave her legs like most girls her age, and the others called her "Monkey Girl." She came to view herself as dumb (especially in math) and ugly and would say these things about herself out loud to others. When asked why she did this, as it often resulted in more teasing or name-calling, she explained that it was what the other kids thought and she wanted them to know she thought so too. She wanted to be like them so that maybe they would be nicer to her. She had no friends and didn't expect to have any. She worried about her future. She began to sink into hopelessness and despair, becoming more and more depressed.*

As Rachael's story illustrates, the effect of the information processing disability on these children's learning and social competency is notable, and not only in the obvious ways we have seen, affecting functioning. It also has a significant effect on self-esteem, or the way in which the child views himself. The frustration of experiencing social interaction like a foreign language and the inability to succeed socially eventually wear the child down. Over time, social failure translates into a loss of self-esteem that adds to the child's sense of confusion and isolation and leads him to avoid social encounters. If social difficulties are left untreated, many people with NLD or AD eventually experience significant depression. It is important to help these children achieve social competency before depression sets in.

The child with NLD or AD has real difficulty understanding the perspective of another person. Remember that these children have never really understood that others are thinking about the same things they think about and, more importantly, that others are thinking about them. This view of the world is, for lack of a better word, self-focused. This is not to imply that these children have a callous disregard for the feelings of others or that their self-focus is self-centered and uncaring. On the contrary, they are very caring; they are just unaware that the views or needs of other people impact them. This awareness is not simple, and it does not seem to come easily for these children.

## Looking in a Mirror vs. Looking out a Window

A self-focused perspective is similar to looking into a mirror and seeing only yourself. This worldview is quite different than looking out a window and seeing the world and the people in it. In some ways, it is as if children with NLD or AD are stuck looking into a mirror and our task is to get them to look out the window.

Addressing these children's issue of self-focus and their inability to take another person's perspective is a valuable goal, but in practice this is difficult at best. If anything should be clear at this point, it is that the three major areas of difficulty these children experience (visual-spatial and sensory integration, organization and executive function, and social skills) are all interconnected and affect each other. Given that these children are actually taking in information in a distorted way, it follows that any attempts to address their self-focus must be built on other interventions addressing their organizational deficits and visual-spatial deficits. Working on one area without addressing the other two is unlikely to be successful.

## Noticing Other People

When a baby in his father's arms points to the moon and looks to his father, he is communicating with his father without language. The language of nonverbal communication—gestures, facial expressions, posture, and body language—is ultimately based on a language of the eyes. Looking at the eyes of other people starts in infancy when we gaze into our mother's eyes. Our first and fundamental type of communication and interaction transcends spoken language. It is interesting to note, as Simon Baron-Cohen does (1995), that even blind children will use language that denotes seeing, asking others to "look" at something—an act these children have never been able to do. The social meanings of looking and seeing are far-reaching, and the fact that children with NLD or AD have a disruption in visual-spatial processing puts them at a significant disadvantage in interpreting the social communications that are based on seeing.

## Learning to Notice

The first and most obvious aspect of social competency training for any child is practice in noticing things the child would not normally attend to. For example, a child with NLD or AD is more likely to hear a series of facts in a conversation with his mother than to notice that her hair, facial expression, or even tone of voice is different. Further, given the limits of the child's information processing ability, a long monologue by his mom is likely to be lost—jumbled and forgotten in the messy storage system of the child's brain. If his mom repeats what she has said over and over to remind the child, this doesn't help matters (especially for his mother, who will probably become increasingly frustrated).

The child's inability to read the nuances of communication are very likely to lead to social rejection by peers and increasing isolation. A look of sarcasm conveyed with the eyes, the knowledge that other kids have about how close to stand to someone, or the anger conveyed by a teacher's tone of voice are all nuances of communication the child with NLD or AD will miss. These nuances of communication will need to be taught. Again, it is important to remember that language level (how well a child can produce language) does not equal communication level (how well a child can communicate). We need to help these children develop their communication level and, thus, their social competency. The first thing the child needs to learn is to notice the important details in communication. Practice in noticing should include both activities and direct instruction to explain the aspects of communication that are missed. Parents and teachers should also create opportunities to help the child acquire the skills he needs to be successful. Some aspects of noticing may seem obvious, others less so. To be successful socially, the child will need to learn to notice the many cues and messages that occur aside from the words people speak. Specific skills to develop include the following:

- Looking at other people's eyes: Ask the child questions about how other people use their eyes to convey information: Are they always the same? What does it mean when eyes are squinted or wide open?

- Noticing where the person is looking: This is an aspect of shared attention, and noticing it assists the child in learning to read cues about meaning and to make assumptions.

- Noticing the expression on the other person's face: Ask the child to guess what it means: Is that an angry look, a worried one, a happy one?

- Looking at how someone is standing or sitting: Ask the child what he can guess about what the other person is thinking based on posture and other aspects of body language.

- Noticing how people walk—their speed and flow of movement: Ask the child what fast walking might mean as opposed to slow, meandering walking.

## Simple Social Skills

Beyond noticing the behavior of other people, certain skills are critical to social success. Most people learn these skills without overt teaching, just by being a member of the social group. However, those with NLD or AD may need direct instruction in these skills. Though the following important skills are categorized as "simple," that doesn't mean they're easy, it just means they're less complicated than other social skills discussed later in the chapter.

- Reading the facial expressions and gestures of others.

- Knowing their own facial expressions and what they are conveying to others.

- Having a sense of what is likely to happen in social situations: Predicting outcomes lessens the novelty of interactions, making them less stressful and more easily coped with.

- Keeping in mind the presence and interest of others in conversation: These children need to learn that conversation is not a monologue.

- Learning to give as well as learning to take: This is another aspect of taking the perspective of the other person. Giving and taking involve attention, compliments, and feedback.

To develop and regularly implement these skills, the child will need many years of training. Certain activities, described below, can be helpful, but the best recommendation is to get involved with an experienced clinician—a psychologist, educational therapist, or behavioral pediatrician—who can manage the many aspects of training the child in these social skills. This person will be a valuable asset over the years to come.

## Activities to Help Develop Simple Social Skills

Videotape the child making a series of facial expressions—happy, sad, angry, worried, scared, bored, and so on—and have the child watch himself. Do the same with other children and adults and have the child guess what the feeling is. This task can also be accomplished without a video camera: Simply have the child make the face you request while looking into a handheld mirror. Polaroid photos can be very helpful, too. As the child practices and gets better at making the correct expressions, the photos provide a history of his progress. There are commercially made drawings of cartoon characters supposedly making facial expressions that match the word listed below the drawing. Although useful early in the development of social skills, the drawings are hardly accurate representations, and many children (and adults, too) would be hard-pressed to guess what emotion some of those cartoons are supposed to be depicting.

Turn off the sound on the TV during a video or movie and work with the child to decipher what is happening. This will require the child to read cues in the actors' facial expressions, posture, gestures, and other body language.

Read a story and ask, "What do you think would happen next?" Discuss how important it is to have some way to predict what is likely to happen next. Help the child develop an awareness of which cues can help give him an idea of what will happen next. Learning to read behavioral cues and predict actions makes social situations much less mysterious.

Create a book of situations, with different chapters for the different social demands the child will deal with that month, such as school, church, scouts, or a birthday party. Help the child predict what will happen and develop a plan for what he is likely to need to do in these situations. *Comic Strip Conversations* (1994), by Carol Gray, presents a formal program that is a more involved and well-developed variation on this idea. This is a very well-thought-out program that is especially useful for clinicians and school psychologists to use in schools to help children deal with the social pressures they encounter there.

Notice and work with animals. This is often less stressful and more fun for the child than practicing social situations with other people. Ask the child what it might mean when a dog wags his tail or cowers down and puts his ears back. Contact with animals can be a wonderful way to work on empathy and reading social cues, as animals are predictable and engaging. Because they are pack animals, dogs have social behaviors that are easily described and learned, making the experience particularly rewarding for the child. Plus, most dogs are forgiving of the mistakes a trainer makes and are happy to see the child. In fact, working with dogs can be such an effective intervention that it's part of the curriculum at the Orion Academy.

## Dog Training for Practice in Nonverbal Social Interactions

At the Orion Academy, a two-part program in dog training that occurs over two years is a required course for all students. The course is based on the idea that animals in general, and dogs in particular, have meaningful and complex social interactions that are nonverbal. In many ways, animals are actually easier to understand than people, so they offer a model for learning how to deal with people. Part 1 teaches about pack mentality, social hierarchy among dogs, and the "language" of dogs (body language, that is), and students are introduced to aspects of breed behavior and temperament. Many of these concepts are new to students and are discussed in terms of both dog training and human interactions. The class sets the stage for the development of good ownership skills and beginning training skills. Part 2 teaches students to actually train dogs in good manners and obedience. Students learn to understand the meanings of dog behaviors and use this knowledge to develop skills as trainers and handlers. To be successful as dog trainers, students must learn to keep track of the signals they, as handlers, are giving and at the same time read the signals the dog is giving. These are important skills that translate well into day-to-day life and increase the child's chances of social success.

Work with animals requires the guidance of a knowledgeable person, and dogs must be chosen for temperament and breeding. It is not recommended that a child with NLD or AD be left alone at any time to deal with an unknown dog or even a family pet that is not screened. In addition to work with dogs, a number of programs for these children include horsemanship. Horses, like dogs, are unlikely to be hurt by the child's mistakes. Plus, they are smart and generally enjoy being around people. Again, trained adults are necessary for these interventions to be successful, but because the benefits of these programs are becoming clear, they are gaining momentum. Such programs should become increasingly available in coming years.

## The Concept of the Other

Children with NLD or AD need to develop an automatic response to check themselves—to notice what they are doing and the response they are getting. Becoming more aware of others reduces the tendency for these children to be seen as aloof and arrogant and helps them learn the language of communication that their peers take for granted. They need to develop a sense of the other person in the interaction—an awareness of their audience. This brings us back again to noticing—specifically, practice in noticing—the following about other people:

- Their mood or feelings: For the child with NLD or AD, the fact that others may notice that someone is sad without asking the person seems magical, like mind reading.

- Their expressions: Does it fit the mood the person is conveying through words and actions?

- Their posture: What does the person's body language convey?

- Their spatial relationship to others: Is the other person close or far away? Does the other person seem comfortable with the proximity of the child?

- Tone of voice: Is the other person's voice loud or soft? Is the person's tone varied or more of a monotone? Ask the child to compare his speech to the other person's. Does his speech have variations of pitch and volume?

- Speed of speech: What might it mean if another person's speech is fast or slow?

- Word choices: Is the speaker choosing words that are appropriate for peers when with peers and for other audiences (teachers, parents, work colleagues) when addressing them?

## Developing Interventions for Simple Social Skills

There are many simple ways to develop opportunities for practice in social skills both at school and at home, but a couple of general guidelines prevail. All children are more likely to work on and look at their own issues when working with someone other than a parent. No matter how close the relationship—and often because it is so close—children are reluctant to be totally open about their worries or their behavior with a parent. Social skills training is best undertaken and directed by a psychologist, whether at school or in private practice. Parents should be involved in supporting the program through home practice. Speech and language therapists are highly effective for working on pragmatic language development, in both individual and small group sessions. When parents take the time to develop a qualified team of professional and caring adults to help their child, the benefits are greater and the changes more significant.

For each skill or behavior to be taught, direct instruction will be needed. The model for teaching social skills follows these steps:

1. Explain verbally exactly what the child needs to do, developing a script, or set of verbal directions, if needed. For example, you'll use language to help the child understand what you mean when you say "facial expressions."

2. Model, or demonstrate, the behavior or present an example of it using a picture, a video, or role-playing so the child can see both how it should be done and how it should not be done.

3. Ask the child to explain to you what you just did. If you are using a script, ask the child to learn the script.

4. Ask the child to model the behavior.

5. Develop a way to add the behavior to the child's memory. The type of information you're teaching will determine how best to help the child remember it. As an example, help the child remember that all behaviors for greeting and meeting people belong together by teaching them together, perhaps as a list or a rhyme the child can use as a mnemonic device, or by creating a book for the child. *Comic Strip Conversations* (Gray 1994) could be of help here as a way to create stories for the child's own situations.

6. The child must practice, practice, practice—with the adult, with peers, and in groups.

## Building a Foundation of Social Skills

There are many social skills to learn and many aspects of any social encounter; that's why this process is so hard. But a few skills that are central to success can be identified. Recall the pragmatic language review form used at the Orion Academy, which was presented in chapter 2. This form actually outlines many of the skills central to social success—skills most children master with time. In developing a social skills program for the child with NLD or AD, assessment of the child's social deficits and strengths should come first. Following that assessment, a coordinated and planned program of social training needs to be instituted. This program should take into account the developmental level of the child. The expectations for an eight-year-old in the lunchroom at school are very different from those for a seventeen-year-old in a similar situation. Keep in mind that skills need to build upon each other. You wouldn't ask someone who has never driven a car to drive through Los Angeles. You would teach the many parts of driving, then offer supervised practice. Only after the person has experienced success in situations that are less challenging and less stressful would you expect that they could drive on the freeways of Los Angeles.

Let's take a look at how the child with NLD or AD can be taught some of the important "simple" social skills. Regardless of the specific skill or training method, always make an effort to compliment the child when he does it correctly. Too often we are quick to point out when something is wrong and forget to provide positive feedback when it is correct.

- Looking into the eyes of another person when communicating: This conveys attention. It will also help ensure that the child is actually seeing the facial expression of the person who is speaking. Cueing the child to remember to do this will be necessary to help him remember, whether he is practicing with a video or in a small group.

- Using facial expressions that are appropriate to the content of the words spoken: Activities such as matching faces to statements on an audiotape and peer-to-peer practice are helpful in building this skill.

- Noticing facial expressions, body language, and physical proximity of oneself and others: This training is best started in one-on-one practice sessions, moving gradually to work in small groups. Keeping track of all three areas (expressions, body language, and proximity) is much more difficult than tracking any of the three alone, and increasing the size of the group will increase the complexity.

- Speaking clearly, not mumbling: For some children, mumbling is related to motor issues and needs to be dealt with in speech therapy; for others it is just a bad habit.

- Using varied tone of voice and appropriate volume: The child with NLD or AD frequently misjudges how loud he is speaking and forgets to make what he is saying interesting to the audience. Videotaping and audiotaping offer great feedback for the child.

- Choosing topics for conversation that are appropriate to the setting (home, school, or other community settings) and appropriate to the audience (peers, adults, family, strangers): For many children, part of this training will involve developing separate lists of topics: one for school, one for extracurricular activities or other social settings, and one for home. These lists can be a safety net for the child in new or challenging situations. Practice with the child's speech therapist or psychologist in a small-group setting to increase the child's feelings of mastery. This will help him learn to call up the appropriate list on the spur of the moment.

- Maintaining a topic in conversation: The child needs to learn to keep the flow on the topic and provide the necessary information so others understand what he is talking about.

- Being flexible about changing topics in conversation: Often, these children will revert back to a preferred topic and need to be reminded of what others wish to talk about. This takes practice and feedback from adults.

- Asking for help when needed: It's hard to know when the child needs help, as he may not tell anyone, but providing the help he needs and complimenting him on asking for help are probably the best ways to increase this behavior.

- Other conversational skills: These are best taught by a psychologist or speech therapist in practice sessions. Parents and family members can help by reminding the child to use the skills he's learning in specific situations. Key skills include the following:

  - Taking turns in a conversation, not monopolizing it.

  - Waiting to be acknowledged or called on before speaking in a group or in class.

  - Introducing oneself to others appropriately.

  - Using appropriate conversational pleasantries, such as "please," "thank you," "It's nice to meet you," and "How are you?"

Teens with NLD or AD should have some ability in all of the skills listed here before they enter high school, and to that end, all children with NLD or AD need to have a program in place that addresses or will address, when age-appropriate, these skills. The complex social skills discussed in the following section should also be part of that program. For most (if not all) of these children, a weekly social skills group will not be enough. Their environment as a whole needs to support the development of these important skills. Often, it is helpful to arrange for a peer model for the child. In younger grades, working with a buddy designated by the teacher can be very successful. This buddy offers a daily model for the child to emulate while at the same time providing practice at social interaction. But by third grade, the buddy is often less interested in being responsible for the child with NLD or AD—and frankly, it isn't the buddy's job to spend recess chaperoning this classmate.

For children with greater needs in the social sphere, who also are prone to be "lost in space" and totally disorganized, assigning them an aide is often a necessary intervention. The use of an aide has its difficulties, as mentioned before, and aides should be used carefully within the context of a plan that will eventually eliminate their services. When any modification is developed for the child, the overall plan must include a transition toward independence and away from that service or modification. If the child will need the service forever, the plan should consider how the modification will be implemented in adulthood.

Early involvement with peers and classroom education in tolerating diversity is extremely important for all children, not just the student with NLD or AD. Yet this component of education—an intervention at the level of the entire class or even the entire school—has limited usefulness if it's not followed up with direct teaching for the child with NLD or AD. The responsibility for effecting change, the power to have control over his own happiness and success, needs to eventually rest with the individual and not depend on the environment he is in. This is an extremely important concept. As mentioned before, the goal is not to create an individual whose happiness and success are dependent on being provided an ideal environment; the goal is to help the child mature into a self-sufficient and functioning adult who owns his own feelings and feels some level of competency in social relationships.

## Developing Skills in Social Competency

The process of developing skills in social competency usually occurs over many years. As discussed earlier, even infants have skills in social connection and "mind reading" (Baron-Cohen 1995). The first skills to be acquired are simple and straightforward. For example, when someone says "hello," you are supposed to respond in a certain manner, looking at the other person and saying "hello" back. But soon even simple skills have more complex expectations associated with them. Greeting an adult entails a different set of expectations in regard to words, tone, and physical proximity than greeting an age-mate. Early, simple skills are added to over time, and increasingly complex social interactions are expected by adulthood. For the child with NLD or AD, movement from the simple skills that can be memorized to the complex skills expected in adolescence and adulthood is a difficult task. Training and intervention in the language of social skills is a primary need for any program for these children.

Two very helpful books provide an excellent program in working with children on developing the social skills described here: *Helping the Child Who Doesn't Fit In* (Nowicki and Duke 1992) and *Teaching Your Child the Language of Social Success* (Duke, Nowicki, and Martin 1996). These books offer ideas that parents can use and activities that can be incorporated into school programs and specialized activity groups.

## Complex Social Skills

Like mathematics, social skills build on each other. Once a skill is learned, it can be added to, making increasingly complex social interactions possible. Most children handle complex interactions every day, holding a conversation, for instance. Conversations have purposes or goals, and the goal of one person may be different than the goal of the other. This means that getting needs met is one area of conversation that can be simple or complex. Asking your mother for more potatoes at dinner might spark a dialogue: For example, she might ask if you like the potatoes. If you don't want to talk more, you can convey this in tone, body language, and facial expression as well as in words. While this seems like a simple interaction, it gets complicated if you realize that your mom worked hard on the potatoes. You want to compliment her, and you guess she is asking if you like the potatoes to see whether you will compliment her. So you do. Now the interaction is more complex, and your goal has shifted from getting more potatoes to wanting to make sure your mother feels complimented.

Most of us never think about the layers of communication and meaning in conversations or interactions, and sometimes a lot is communicated even though no words are exchanged. Children with NLD or AD are at a great disadvantage here. If something as simple as wanting more potatoes at dinner can spin off so easily into other directions, just imagine what can happen with the many, many other interactions we engage in daily. Talk about multitasking! We are constantly expected to organize multiple concepts and read different levels of communication at the same time.

Conversational skills and other, more complicated social skills develop over time, using the simple skills already described in combination and in sequence. Most children with NLD or AD will need the same intensity of direct teaching for the following complex skills as they need for simple social skills:

- Being aware of the interest of the listener (not rambling on one topic). This is a complex skill as it involves a combination of many skills: noticing verbal and nonverbal cues, organizing thoughts, modulating tone of voice, and flexibility about conversational topics, to name a few.

- Introducing and discussing topics clearly, keeping the context and the connections between topics clear to the listener.

- Expressing relevant information and expressing it concisely. This requires organizing what one wants to say and focusing on that.

- Attending to comments the other person has made, responding to those comments, and allowing the flow of conversation to shift, if necessary. This last is a very important and often overlooked skill.

- Understanding sarcasm and using it correctly.

- Understanding metaphor and analogy and using them correctly.

- Understanding teasing and using it appropriately and in an age-appropriate manner. Not all teasing is bad, and learning how to tease friends is an art that can be acquired.

- Letting go of an argument. To do this, one may have to "agree to disagree" with the other person.

- Learning to interrupt appropriately.

- Learning to ask a speaker to clarify comments appropriately. There is a big difference between "Excuse me, could you explain what you mean by ..." and "That doesn't make any sense."

- Being approachable for conversation. This involves giving off the right cues.

- Initiating original conversation; not talking about the same thing over and over.

## Ongoing Problems of Self-Focus

The idea of looking into a mirror rather than out a window is a way of understanding the problem of social interactions for children with NLD or AD. It is not often discussed in the literature, but these children can appear arrogant and self-focused, especially as they get older. Their insistence on rigid rules and presentation of themselves as "experts" does little to increase their appeal in the eyes of their peers, and it can be annoying for family members. Well-meaning professionals and parents have often unwittingly supported these dysfunctional behaviors in an attempt to shore up the child's sagging self-esteem. While the need to support self-esteem is real, allowing the child to present himself to others as arrogant or self-important will neither shore up the child's self-esteem nor improve his social skills. Instead, this simply adds another layer of problems to the child's already heavy burden of social deficits. It's a hard line for a parent to walk, helping the child feel good about his strengths in the face of difficulties while not feeding an apparent arrogance and sense of "specialness" that makes the child less likely to make friends.

# Richard's Story

*At fourteen, Richard considers himself an expert on all things related to his computer. He and his father spend many enjoyable hours fiddling with their home system and discussing the modifications they are making and plan to make. For Richard, these are pleasurable hours, and his father tells him over and over how smart and advanced he is in computer knowledge compared to his peers. Yet when Richard goes to school, his peers don't seem to notice how special he is. He acknowledges that many of the other eighth-graders in his class are better at sports, seem more organized, and have more friends, but he knows as much as they do about history and he is sure he knows more about computers.*

*When he talks about his computer and the games he has downloaded, some students seem interested for a little while. But eventually they all seem to drift away, and Richard finds himself alone. He likes to give advice to the other kids to show them how much he knows, but there isn't a lot of opportunity to do so. And when there is, his advice is hardly welcomed. One morning, he came into his homeroom early to find his teacher, Mr. Smith, discussing his computer problems with another teacher. Richard intruded uninvited into the conversation and began to give Mr. Smith instructions on how to fix his problem. When Mr. Smith, who was annoyed by this behavior, replied, "Thank you, Richard, but I have it under control," and turned back to the other teacher, Richard interrupted again to say, "Well, actually, Mr. Smith, I don't think you do." Needless to say, Mr. Smith didn't find Richard's comment helpful or appropriate.*

## Expert Status and Arrogance

Reliance on expert status is a common behavior for individuals with NLD or AD. They tend to have circumscribed areas of interest their entire lives, and they develop a certain expertise on the topics they have focused on for so long. It is important to note that although the child may have years of interest in insects, he may actually have very narrow knowledge within that interest, perhaps having no knowledge beyond the specialized area of ants. Talking about this area of expertise has been pleasurable for the child in the past and, like all of us, he will seek to feel good whenever possible. Unfortunately, the child has little understanding of the effect this has on the way other people see him. Sometimes, this disorder is intensified by well-meaning professionals or parents repeatedly telling the child how "smart" he is. Because most of these children are literal, concrete thinkers, the child will probably interpret this literally, believing that he is very smart overall and repeating this fact to others, whether it is appropriate or not. Problems are particularly likely to occur when this expert status is pulled out and wielded like a weapon, which often happens when the child is feeling threatened or confused.

Telling classmates he is smarter than they are or interrupting every conversation with "Well, actually" before launching into his ideas on the subject can make others view the child with NLD or AD as arrogant. In many ways, that view could be accurate, especially if the child has never had help taking the perspective of other people or if he has built up years of anger at the way peers have rejected him. These children are just as capable of being mean as any other child is. When these children feel threatened or confused, their limited social repertoire sets them up to use what they know—information and language. They have few weapons or defenses, and these are what they know best. This aspect of NLD or AD is often ignored—the tendency to use an arrogant, better-than-you-are presentation to cover for feeling out of control and confused. This behavior gives the child a false sense of momentary control and of getting back at the kids who have been mean to him, but this approach never pays off in the long run. The child doesn't really have control of the social situation, and worse, these children tend to use the "expert" stance even when they aren't threatened. This may be a preemptive strike of sorts; one NLD teen has explained that he assumes peers will reject him, so he starts out by presenting himself as above them to reject them before they reject him.

Unfortunately, many of these children and teens cannot tell when a peer is reaching out to them, so they often respond to gestures of friendship with this same arrogance. With some of these children, a peer must have a strong desire to make friends in order to succeed. It is helpful for teachers, clinicians, and parents to point out to the child when he is "being the expert" to assist the child with changing the way he interacts with others. The earlier this sort of intervention begins, the better chance the child has of developing a range of relationship responses by adolescence. It will also be advantageous for these children to learn to notice when someone wants to be their friend and to respond appropriately.

## Negativity

For reasons that are far from clear, children and teens with NLD or AD are plagued with a pervasive negative response style. For some, this manifests as an immediate "no" to anything new. For others, it goes beyond that to viewing others negatively and even to affecting their sense of the future. This negativity is a turnoff for other people and a source of ongoing frustration for teachers and parents. For people involved with these "negative Nellies," it is essential to remember that you are not the one causing the negativity and that you cannot fix it. The child must be reminded not to be so negative, as they are unaware of how they are coming across. It helps to point out that, in many cases, this will have a positive effect on relationships and interactions. Sometimes it is best to remind them that when they wish to make a negative comment in public, to "think it; don't say it." Negativity can become a more serious problem in some cases, developing into depression and a sense of hopelessness. In those instances, it is important to seek professional help before the child or teen becomes overwhelmed by his inner thoughts.

## Fear of Letting Go

Because it seems to these children that other people have so much more information on so many day-to-day things, letting go of what expert status they have is a lot to ask of them. The challenge for parents and professionals is to help the child strike a balance, not to try to eradicate the child's coping behaviors without offering more appropriate replacements. In some ways, the need to cling to an area of expert knowledge is not unlike a small child's need for a security blanket or thumb sucking. Although such coping strategies provide security, it is very important for healthy adult functioning that all children gradually learn to reduce or eliminate their dependence on these things. It cannot be done quickly. For example, taking a computer away from a child who has relied on computers for years as an extension of himself will be devastating. His self-esteem is tied up in that machine, and moving him away from that position will take time. Conversely, it is not a good idea to allow these children unlimited time for their focused interests.

Try to help the child broaden his interests. A boy who compulsively readjusts the preferences on his computer could be urged (or even required by his parents) to do more with computers than just work on his own system. For example, he could set up a computer system for a neighbor or for a nursing home. He would not necessarily have to work with the people in these places, if that is too stressful, but he could spend time volunteering in the area of expertise where he is so comfortable. Help the child push his limits a little, and you might be pleasantly surprised. If you never expect the child to do things or take responsibility, he never will.

You might try to help the child broaden his interests by gradually generalizing from his specific area of focus, for example, from an obsessive focus on steam trains to learning about the history of trains in the United States to eventually developing an interest in the history of the westward movement in general. If this doesn't seem to work, try to add interests. Expose the child to different activities and ideas, limiting the time spent on the obsessive activity. If computers are the obsession, limit daily computer time. Insist that other things must be done to earn time on the computer, and stick to that rule. For example, to earn an hour on the computer, the child would need to do two of the following:

- Greeting Mom and Dad in an appropriate way in the morning and afternoon

- Bathing and grooming

- Brushing teeth after each meal

- Feeding and walking the dog

- Making pleasant dinner conversation

Parents can make checklists of these activities. When the child does one of the activities, he checks it off, then presents the checklist, almost like a ticket, for computer time.

As the child matures, the checklist should contain activities that make more complex social demands on the child, such as participation in church, clubs, or after-school activities, or inviting a friendly peer over. It is very important to remember that although these children need some access to their security blanket (whatever that may be), if they are allowed to become immersed in their own world, it becomes harder and harder for them to participate in the world of other people.

## ■ Dashell's Story

*Dashell loved history and would try to answer every question his fifth-grade teacher asked about American history. He would raise his hand and call out, "I know, I know," or sometimes just blurt out the answer before anyone else could. Other students were getting annoyed and would argue and become angry with him, seeing him as a conceited show-off. He had no idea he was seen this way, nor did his mom, until a parent told her that the other students disliked Dashell's style in class. His mother and the teacher talked to him openly about the problem, and he was surprised and worried; he certainly wasn't trying to make the other kids dislike him. Together, they devised a plan that was partly directed at Dashell and partly at the entire class. Dashell and any other students who wanted to could sign up as contestants in a twice-a-week classroom version of history* Jeopardy. *(A side benefit is that this activity involves preplanning, a skill that children with NLD or AD usually need to work on developing.) The teacher specified the categories, choosing areas she knew Dashell would excel in, as well as choosing areas where other students would do well. The students played in teams, each getting the experience of being the expert and being on the team. Dashell became a valuable and highly sought-after team member, and he learned to delay his need for attention and to listen to his classmates and value their responses. And he had fun!*

## Reliance on Rigidity

Left to their own devices, children with NLD or AD will go through life like a train on a track: one way, straight ahead, never varying, and avoiding the unexpected. But because life doesn't allow any of us to live that way, these children need to learn to move off the track. Telling the child—and showing him through many experiences over many years—that flexibility is a good thing and not to be feared names the needed skill and helps the child learn it. Compliment the child whenever he is flexible, bending and changing and trying new things.

Parents need to work to help these children develop skills at surviving in the world. Plan to take them places they might enjoy, such as restaurants, on public transportation, and to age-appropriate entertainment. During these experiences, the pressure to read so many pieces of sensory and social information at once is tiring and can be stressful, so don't schedule too many trips or too many social encounters all at once. Increase expectations as the child gets older. As with training muscles, if you don't use social skills, you'll lose them; children with NLD or AD need to train for life.

# Teasing and Being Teased

Perhaps the single most damaging effect of NLD and AD is the effect these deficits have on the child's social competency and on how others treat him. Certainly, learning is impacted and, without help, the child's academic success can be compromised, but social rejection has devastating consequences. Teasing is part of life, right or wrong. There is hardly anyone who has not been subjected to teasing at some point. Friendly teasing is often part of a rite of passage in some families; when Uncle Joe teases you, it shows you are an accepted member of the family. It is also a common and accepted mode of exchange between teenagers. But children with NLD or AD are so bad at teasing that even when they try to tease playfully, the experience usually isn't positive. Eventually they just stop trying.

Playful teasing among peers is different from the painful and confusing encounters these children experience on the playground or in social groups. From a very young age, they are often the subject of comments and remarks from peers. This is partly because, as a group, their unusual behavior calls attention to them. Their gait, their odd manner of talking (the "little professor" speech), and their poor motor skills all mark them as different. In addition, the fact that many of these children are unaware of ordinary social expectations, much less the behavior that others see as "cool," doesn't help. For example, for some reason, a fair number of children with NLD or AD have the annoying habit of picking their nose in public. This behavior has a compulsive quality to it, and the child will sit in class picking his nose, much to the disgust of classmates. The teasing that predictably follows does not deter the child, and he continues, losing social status and becoming the focus of ridicule.

## Teaching Coping and Survival Skills

Not all children with NLD or AD who are teased have a direct or observable behavior that can be addressed (like nose picking). Often the teasing stems from their misguided attempts to engage others, usually through their "expert" talking style or just through not getting the flow of peer interactions. As mentioned earlier, it is important to provide as many healthy and supportive social situations as possible. It is also important to protect children from abuse or ridicule. Yet it will never be possible to control all the situations the child will encounter. It's better to equip the child with coping skills that involve strategies for looking at how the child interacts as well as clear guidelines for reading a situation and judging if he needs to leave. Knowing how and when to leave a group is just as difficult as knowing how to enter one. Unfortunately, many of these children wait too long before leaving a social encounter gone bad. Because of their poor judgment and limited ability to read social cues, they can easily get themselves into hurtful or even dangerous situations. Social skills training should include teaching the child ways to get out of situations that make him uncomfortable.

Knowing how to avoid situations that are likely to be problematic is another valuable skill. For example, if the bathroom in the C wing of the high school is the hangout for the "tough" group of boys at lunch, teachers and parents need to explicitly tell the teen with NLD or AD that he shouldn't go into that bathroom at that time. The social skills needed to handle potential problems in that situation are more than this boy has at his disposal. Teaching survival skills also involves teaching children that not everyone is necessarily going to be a friend. This teaching requires that children with NLD or AD are not so protected that they never learn how to survive. The more they get out and learn scripts for handling life, the better able they will be to live it.

A word of caution is in order: As easy as it may be to say that you must teach survival skills, there is a very fine line to walk here. The challenge for parents and professionals is to strike a very important balance, providing a safe and supportive environment for these children without overprotecting them from life. A safe and appropriate educational environment is a must; this is not a need that can be ignored. And the child will need to be allowed to try things, to succeed and to fail socially, with the knowledge that his family is always there for support.

## Putting It All Together

For the child with NLD or AD, just as for any child, success finally boils down to putting it all together: all the assessments, the focus on developing social and organizational skills, the experiences and arranged practice. Putting together what we've learned allows us to function independently in the world. It involves defining what makes us happy and setting out to achieve that happiness. Who could ask for more, really? Even for children with no disability, finding happiness is not necessarily an easy thing. This book attempts to show how complex the interactions are that most people take for granted, and how they require a complexity of social and organizational skills. Understanding nonverbal as well as verbal communication is essential for this functioning. According to Duke, Nowicki, and Martin, "only 7 percent of emotional meaning is actually expressed with words" (1996, 7). That means that 93 percent of the emotional meaning in the way people communicate is expressed in ways other than spoken language. To miss 93 percent of the meaning in an interaction is a serious deficit. With this in mind, it should be clear just how much hard work these children and their families must go through to develop skills others take for granted.

Learning how to use words to their advantage is a goal most children with NLD or AD can eventually reach. Learning how to connect the nonverbal parts of communication with the verbal is also something they can eventually accomplish. This work is necessary and central to healthy development—just as central as academic learning. Being accepted by peers and adults in your community goes a long way toward fostering healthy self-esteem. Instead of a false sense of self-worth, created artificially by the adults in the child's life, developing real competency in social situations is a valuable and reasonable goal. All of the advice in this book can play an important role in helping develop this competency. In addition, these children need to develop a total package of skills that defines who they are and reflects the view of themselves they want others to have. This view evolves as a direct result of learning to take another person's perspective. It is a natural extension of the sense of self, and these children need help making this extension.

Who am I, and how do I want others to think of me? This is a hard question for most children with NLD or AD—and for most teens, regardless of disability—unless they have been working directly on this idea. To answer these questions, a person must first think about himself as he relates to others, and he also has to think about others as they relate to him. Most children never think about this idea as consciously as every teen with NLD or AD will need to. Answering these questions is important and complicated, and the ability to do so develops out of the hard work described in this book.

## Being "Cool"

Ask any child what "cool" is and he will be hard-pressed to define it in words. More likely, the child will give examples of what is and is not cool. In essence, "cool" is knowing and using certain words, tone, flow, and rhythm in communication. It is being aware of and in tune with the situation and interacting appropriately with those around you. In clinical terms, this awareness is often referred to as synchronicity. Developing a synchronicity with those around you suggests you know how to use nonverbal communication—that you can read much of that 93 percent of communication that is not spoken. Developing synchronicity makes you cool.

## Grooming

Another level of communication is conveyed through things like posture, tone of voice, rate of speech, and general body language. An aspect of that body language that appears to be a particular problem for children and teens with NLD or AD is grooming. As mentioned earlier, poor hygiene appears to partly be a result of the sensory integration difficulties these children experience. The feel of water, shampoo, or a toothbrush is so disturbing to them that they learn to avoid the experience. The fact that they cannot smell themselves or notice that their clothes are stained and rumpled from days of wear complicates matters. So parents, professionals, and other caretakers need to begin early teaching the child that the social conventions of our culture require a certain level of grooming with which they must comply.

Be creative: Pants or skirts with an elastic waist can usually be found to accommodate any situation. Set a schedule for bathing and hair washing and stick to it; this will develop into a routine and become easier. Keep in mind that if the child's hair is washed often (say, every two days), the job will go more quickly, which will in turn increase the likelihood of the child's adapting to the sensation. Experiment with different shampoos and soaps, and make bathing fun whenever possible. Because older children and teens should be bathing and grooming themselves, with them you'll have to go with the old standby: washing earns them privileges and rewards they desire. It is necessary to teach this life lesson—that stinky people are not easily accepted by peers.

Here's an example of how this lesson can be reinforced: A parent refused to drive her son, John, to school in the morning because he had slept in his clothes for three days in a row and had not bathed. When he got up in the same messy, rumpled outfit for the third day, she told him that she wouldn't take him to school until he had showered and changed. He refused, stating he would just stay home. His mother called the school, got his teacher on the phone, explained the situation, then put John on the phone. The teacher told John that she understood the problem and what his choice was, but that he would be counted as cutting class that day, and that she hoped to see him the next day. His mother told him to go back to his room after he had eaten and that he would have no TV or computer privileges because he cut school. Later in the day, his mother reminded him of the need to shower and be dressed in clean clothes in the morning and said she would not get into a debate with him about it. This was the rule and she intended to stick to it. The next morning, he was showered and dressed in clean clothes.

This is not to imply all such encounters will go so well, and some children may need more than one experience to get the message. But a few tactics seem to increase success:

■ Be clear and concise in your expectations. Don't say one thing on one day and another thing a different day. In the example just given, the mother sent a clear message: You need to shower every two days and wear clean clothes to school. Clean clothes were defined as having been worn no more than two days and not slept in.

- Stick to your guns in a calm and businesslike manner. There is no reason to scream and yell. Remember that the child is responding to his internal state and the learning he has already taken in. In most cases, that learning has been that the parent will give in. But if the child stinks, he needs to bathe or he cannot continue to enjoy privileges. It is a logical consequence: The smell or inappropriate clothing disturbs others, and for these children, learning the effect they have on others is very important. Remembering the importance of this lesson may help you stand firm.

- Solicit support from an important person in the child's world, like the child's teacher in the example above. This was a valuable intervention, as the teacher presented a logical consequence the child understood: His record would reflect that he cut school. The teacher was not angry, nor was she pleading or cajoling; like the mother, she was clear and businesslike, explaining what the consequence was.

- Remind but don't nag. Offer ideas about how the child can do what he needs to. Offer options for shampoo, soap, or bathing methods to help the child find what works best for him.

Compromise and negotiation may also be needed in the matter of clothing. Most children with NLD or AD have a style they prefer. It may be compulsive, like a jacket that never comes off, even in hot weather. There is room for personal style unless the child attends a school with a uniform, in which case he'll probably be required to comply. If there's no such restriction, having five different pairs of sweatpants for school may be boring, but it will be clean and neat, and it can allow the child to dress in a manner that is a compromise between his sensory needs and society's demands.

## Issues of Adolescence

For older children and teens, the issues of coolness and grooming are a bit more complicated. Given that most teens with NLD or AD are behind their peers developmentally, they often don't even notice what clothes are considered cool. For some parents, especially if the child with NLD or AD is their first child, the tendency is to keep dressing the child younger than is appropriate for his age or grade. This may be because the child doesn't request different clothes or because parents just don't think about it, but a fourteen-year-old in Gymboree shirts (even if he can fit into them) is not a good idea. As a rule of thumb, middle-of-the-road dress makes the most sense for these children. That is, it would not be a good idea to dress them in eye-catching or seductive clothing, including expensive footwear for boys, even if that's what all the child's peers are wearing. The attention those clothes may draw may be more than the child can handle. Think simple, comfortable, and easy to wash.

Just because a child has NLD or Asperger's disorder does not mean he will skip being a teenager. The child is just as likely to go through the normal variations of mood and personality as any teen; he just gets to go through adolescence with more baggage. The good news is that, developmentally, most of these teens are slower to become aware of adolescent issues of sexuality, drugs, or rebellion, but these issues will eventually come up. The peer culture we want these children to become a part of is difficult at best, and many of these teens are not prepared to deal with the pressures of sex or drugs. Their logical minds can be a help here. The best approach is to arm them with information and a plan beforehand and, most importantly, to teach them to talk to an adult if they have any questions or confusing encounters. There is no way parents or professionals can prepare the teen for every possible scenario that will come up. Instead, they need to understand that the best course is to get away from confusing situations and talk to adults they trust. As with all teens, drugs and sex do need to be covered in their school curriculum. They need the same tools and information, but it may be best to do this teaching one on one or in smaller group settings, where there is ample opportunity for questions that their peers might find weird or unusual.

The typical adolescent rebellion, or the separation-individuation phase of adolescence, as it is known clinically, is alive and well among teens with NLD or AD. However, it usually happens later (at age seventeen or eighteen, instead of fifteen or sixteen), and it may look different, as teens with NLD or AD are genuinely frightened about what the world has to offer. The idea of leaving home may be overwhelming to them, yet their developmental need to achieve some separation from their parents is real. This confusion can be the source of depression and hopelessness in later adolescence and may need to be addressed professionally.

What is self-esteem but the development of a healthy sense of who we are? No one is perfect, and knowing our limitations along with our strengths helps us accept what is real about who we are. Developing a false sense of oneself is unhealthy and dangerous. This is just as true whether that falseness defines a person as worthless or as extraordinary. For children with NLD or AD, growing up is a difficult and confusing journey. They begin the journey knowing only part of the language and having only part of the map and part of their luggage. Self-esteem comes with the knowledge that they can succeed, even if that success relies on the help of others. There is no question that these children struggle with many deficits, yet they also have strengths that are valuable and worthwhile to them and to those who know them. During the journey they will need help and support to find the missing pieces, but it is ultimately their journey.

# 11

# What Does the Future Hold?

As this book draws to a close, some issues remain untouched and some ideas unfinished. Bear in mind that nonverbal learning disorder is a relatively new diagnosis and that Asperger's disorder is caught in the throes of controversy as the professional community debates the meaning of the diagnosis. Because of these issues, NLD and AD have been underdiagnosed, misdiagnosed, and just plain misunderstood. Exactly what NLD is has yet to be defined in any consistent manner, and as discussed previously, the name itself doesn't do justice to the real issues confronting the individual with this disorder. In this book, Asperger's disorder has been considered in conjunction with NLD. Although it's included in the fourth edition of the *Diagnostic and Statistical Manual of Mental Disorders* (APA 1994), along with diagnostic criteria, and is an accepted diagnosis in both the education and mental health fields, AD is also frequently misdiagnosed, creating confusion and difficulty both in research and in providing programs for these children.

## How NLD, Asperger's, and Other Disorders Relate to One Another

This book presents one view about NLD and AD; there are others. The conclusion presented here is that, although they are separate disorders, NLD and AD should be considered related. Both have in common problems with information processing that affect organizational skills, executive function, sensory integration, working memory, and social competency. As related disorders, they appear to respond to similar interventions and educational programs. The exact nature of the relationship between the two diagnostic categories is unclear, yet it is possible that they belong together on a continuum and that this continuum is separate from the autism spectrum disorders. This idea remains to be proven, and for now, most people still consider AD to be an autism spectrum disorder and often refer to children with AD as autistic or, more recently, as having pervasive development disorder not otherwise specified (PDD-NOS). This book takes issue with that notion, but only future research will provide the knowledge to develop a consistent understanding across different fields of study.

## Not Settling for Just Getting By

To date, professionals working with children with NLD or AD have had to rely on a limited body of information, some of which is primarily anecdotal. However, a slowly growing body of empirical information now backs up the commonsense ideas and observations that much of the past work has been based on. Up to this point, parents have had to settle for interventions that feel like a hit-or-miss approach to addressing their child's needs. Most parents actively seek knowledgeable professionals to help their child reach her highest potential and have the greatest opportunities for the future.

An article in the *New York Times* (Hilts 2001) cited a report by the National Academy of Sciences suggesting that school systems should try to diagnose autism as early as age two. With earlier diagnosis, the number of children identified as having autism and related disorders and needing services at schools will increase, as will the pressure to find effective treatment programs. However, it is likely that many of the children diagnosed with autism and related disorders are actually affected by NLD or AD, and they will need services specific to their disorders. An increase in knowledge regarding both NLD and AD will allow for greater accuracy in diagnosis and, eventually, more appropriate program placement.

# Qualification for Special Education Services

The school system is an essential partner in the success of any child, including those with NLD or AD. Most children with NLD who qualify for special services will do so under categories related to their disability but not specific to NLD. Those with AD often have an easier time qualifying for special education service because Asperger's is recognized as part of the autism spectrum by school districts and autism is one of the twelve handicapping conditions recognized by the federal government.

Every school district in the country is required to provide special education services and meet the guidelines of Public Law 94-142, the federal special education law that went into effect in 1976, which is now known as the Individuals with Disabilities Education Act (IDEA). But each school district is allowed to interpret the law, and many states have additional requirements for qualifying for special education services. As mentioned earlier, parents must take the time to learn about the laws in their state and the guidelines for their district. However, parents can request that their child be evaluated for special education at any time, and that evaluation must occur in a timely manner. If the district concludes that the child does not qualify for special education, the parent may disagree and has recourse through mediation and a fair hearing process. Keep in mind that this can be a long process; many families find the legalities and stress difficult to deal with alone and seek the services of an educational attorney or advocate.

Children diagnosed with AD by a medical doctor or psychologist frequently qualify for special education services early and have an individual education plan (IEP) in place early in their academic life. (An IEP is a legal document that defines the educational program for any child who qualifies for special education services.) This is not necessarily true for children with NLD. The U.S. Department of Education's Office of Special Education and Rehabilitative Services lists twelve categories of special education, including specific learning disabilities, speech and language impairment, other health impairments, and autism. Each school district is responsible for implementing special education programs and is also responsible for providing the services and meeting the goals defined in a student's IEP.

Development of goals for the student and the decisions about appropriate program placement are decided at an IEP meeting, which is attended by parents, school-district personnel, and anyone invited by the parents. The usefulness of the IEP drafted at this meeting is in part a function of who contributes to it. Because of this, it is important for parents to include knowledgeable professionals on their team. Parents have a right to include anyone they wish on the IEP team, and they can present the goals they want included in the IEP. A good assessment comes in handy in determining these goals. Attorneys or other trained advocates for parents are often necessary to set up a working document that is appropriate for the child, especially because many school districts and private schools have limited knowledge about NLD and AD and will need to be provided with information to help develop appropriate programs. If the district is unable to provide the educational environment the child needs to benefit from her education, parents have every reason to seek private services for the child and engage the district in a discussion about how they will provide those services.

NLD is not a recognized diagnostic category, and a diagnosis of NLD will not automatically get a child special education services, such as an IEP. Yet many children with NLD are in serious need of specialized services and program modifications. In some states, services that are not part of an IEP are still available. In California, for example, many children with NLD qualify easily for a 504 plan, a state-mandated program that provides services for students who need modifications to their educational plan but do not qualify for an IEP. The 504 plan is implemented at the discretion of the school district and monitored at the school site. Because it is not an IEP, a 504 plan has limited accountability and, frankly, services are provided at the convenience of the individual school. Most 504 services are things that don't require any additional funds, such as preferential seating in the front of the room but not purchase of a special desk for the child.

Depending on the state and the district, qualification for special education often requires focusing on specific deficits or specific learning disabilities—in written language, mathematics, or pragmatic language development, for example—or on the discrepancy between potential skills (as measured by testing) and actual performance. Many parents of students with NLD have had to resort to the services of an educational attorney to get their child the accommodations and programs needed. But there are success stories, too, along with plenty of district staff who are interested in providing quality programs.

## Effective Program Development

Given that school-age children spend more of their waking time in school than at home with their parents, school programs are very important. The first step in designing a program for a child with NLD or AD is to get a good assessment. From the assessment, teachers and case managers will develop the modifications that are needed, the specific training and teaching tools to be employed, and the additional services to be provided (such as speech therapy, a social skills group, or occupational therapy). Throughout this book, ideas and suggestions for just what that program should look like have been presented, but no two children are alike and each program must take into account the individual needs of the child and the family. However, any program developed on the basis of a competent and complete assessment will likely include the following components:

- Educational modifications

- Occupational therapy or related sensory integration interventions

- Pragmatic language training

- Social skills training

- Family therapy and support

Many children with NLD or AD will also need medication and ongoing work with a psychiatrist and psychologist.

Program placement and related services for children with NLD or AD have been inconsistent at best and ineffective at worst. It is essential that an intervention program be effective. This is really just common sense; if something isn't working, it is hardly worth continuing. The same is true for all aspects of education and any type of treatment. Ineffective treatment for children with NLD or AD can generally be traced to the following basic problems:

- Poor diagnosis of the disorder: The child is often not even receiving the necessary treatments: educational interventions, speech and language therapy, occupational therapy services, or appropriate medication.

- Use of adjunct services in lieu of an overall program approach: A program approach means that the educational curriculum is based on an understanding of the specific needs of the child and that the classroom incorporates needed interventions into the total program. The lack of an overall program approach that has at its core an understanding of the learning differences in NLD and AD is probably the single most significant reason why many well-meaning interventions fail. To provide services once a week or as add-ons, even the so-called push-in services or special lunchtime activities, is more like an afterthought and is unlikely to create any substantial change. If this is all that's available, it's better than nothing, but don't be fooled into thinking this constitutes an appropriate overall program. Interventions for information processing deficits must address three major areas:

    1. Visual-spatial processing and sensory motor integration

    2. Information processing and organizational skills

3. Social skills and pragmatic language development

■ Failure to develop and use modifications that change over time, allowing the child to grow toward independence and self-sufficiency: Children with NLD or AD should have different modifications in eighth grade than in fifth grade, and by high school they should be progressing toward fewer modifications or toward using technology that they can reasonably take into the adult world. Technology can be a great asset for these children, and informed use of new and innovative technology should be a priority in programs designed for them.

Program development should integrate the recommendations in chapters 7 and 8 and appendix B, the Classroom Wish List. Any program for children with NLD or AD must include training in organizational skills and the use of technology as parts of the program, not as add-ons. Recall the whiteboard technology that allows direct transfer of information from the board to the student's laptop. This classroom modification reduces the multitasking required in more advanced courses, allowing the student to focus on the teacher, which leads to greater comprehension and more involvement in the material and classroom discussions.

An appropriate program must take into account in a real way the sensory integration and visual-spatial needs of these children, as described in chapter 9, from development of appropriate educational materials to classroom design and the availability of different sensory integration tools. Teachers and administrators need to make available appropriate desks, chairs, headphones, or other items the students can use to maintain appropriate arousal states.

The curriculum and social climate of the program must incorporate training in social skills, including the approaches described in chapter 10. A central focus of any intervention program for these students must be teaching pragmatic language, self-observation, and the ability to adopt another person's perspective. Traditionally, children with NLD or Asperger's have participated in pragmatic language training programs, usually in small groups run by a certified speech therapist. These groups, similar to social skills groups run by licensed psychologists, focus on developing the child's ability to use language appropriately and teaching behaviors that are socially acceptable. These children's success while in the group is usually high, and the experience is a valuable one. Yet, as mentioned earlier, most professionals find that the skills developed in the group do not generalize easily outside the group.

Training in social skills is usually more successful when seamlessly incorporated into the school day. The program at Orion has clearly demonstrated the success of social skills training when it isn't just an adjunct to the program but rather is included in all aspects of the learning community. A small learning community allows for the development of real friendships—not orchestrated by school staff in friendship groups or assumed to exist because the child is not reporting overt teasing on the playground. It can make a huge difference for the child to find a peer group that respects and admires her for being herself, complete with NLD or AD; this is an amazing and freeing experience that allows social growth not seen in other settings. As discussed in chapter 10, using animals—specifically dog training—has been found to be a successful means of helping these children develop skills in reading nonverbal cues and responding with self-awareness. More research on successful interventions in social competency is needed, as this area of work is difficult and often frustrating for the student and the teacher or therapist.

# The Swing of the Pendulum

Attitudes about education in general and special education in particular seem to follow a cycle that's like the swing of a pendulum. Not only do diagnoses seem to go in and out of fashion, but certain concepts in education seem to go in and out of vogue as well. For the past fifteen years, the pendulum has swung away from specialized education and into the idea of mainstreaming, the concept that children with special needs should be taught in regular classes or in regular education settings as much as possible. This sounds good, and it has had some benefits for the type of children who were being iso-lated and not offered an adequate education in special education. But for a large number of children, the effect of mainstreaming has been a loss of educational supports they needed: specialized classrooms and teachers trained to provide appropriate programs, not just tutoring.

School districts experienced a financial gain by limiting special education services, but for children with NLD or AD, mainstreaming is hardly enough, and real program changes are needed. They need specific types of materials, access to computers, and direct specialized teaching to address their deficits in executive function, organization, pragmatic language, and social skills. Their needs require a different type of thinking than that which prevails in a regular classroom. At times, the services provided have not been in the child's best interest; for example, the use of an aide throughout a child's academic career is hardly preparing the child for increased independence and academic success. The plan for that child needs to include program changes as she matures and direct teaching and technology geared toward helping her become more self-sufficient as a teen.

A lack of appropriate services and of general knowledge about NLD and AD has started the pendulum swinging back. Within the last few years, parents seeking services for their children have fueled the growth of information about and interest in NLD and AD. It is important to find a balance point where the student receives special-ized services that are not limiting socially or academically and that provide an appropriate level of academic challenge and increasing independence. It is time for professionals to get interested and develop programs that specifically address these children's issues. Research on and funding for these programs is badly needed.

## Effects on Families

One of the hardest things this book asks families of children with NLD or AD to do is to allow them to fail. The swing of the pendu-lum that fuels increased services can also protect these children from normal development—from the frustrations and pain of everyday growing up. For a parent, this is clearly the hardest line to walk: allowing some failure, which will support development of inner strength, but protecting the child from becoming overwhelmed by life's trials. Families must find that line on a daily basis and try to walk it as best they can. There is no doubt that these vulnerable children need protection, that they cannot be set out to walk in the wilds alone without training, practice, and preparation. That training for life and practice in surviving is essential, and it is often overlooked. To assume that children with NLD or AD will never be able to use public transportation alone, complete a job interview, or deal with the Department of Motor Vehicles is to assume less of them than they are capable of.

Family members must provide lifelong backup support for the person with NLD or AD. Part of the training these children need is in knowing when to ask for help and when to let others know they can do something themselves. Specifically, they must be educated in their disability and become involved in their own treatment. Developing good working relationships with psychologists, psychiatrists, and medical practitioners will ensure they have more of the support they need. These relationships can continue throughout the person's life and can provide an alternative to parental advice that can be especially valuable during the transition into young adulthood.

## Transition into Adulthood

For those with NLD or AD, the transition into adulthood is probably the least understood part of their lives. Programs have just begun to catch up on services for children and teens, and as yet, there are almost no services for young adults. Special education services end upon graduation from high school; there are no IEPs in college. Colleges and community colleges can offer academic support and certain accommodations under the IDEA law; however, although these services seem promising and are designed with good intentions, they have only mixed success. Nevertheless, until this situation improves, existing postsecondary programs are a potential avenue for help. Web resources like NLDline.com and NLDontheWeb.org offer bulletin boards, chat rooms, and links that allow those with NLD to make connections and suggest things that have worked for them. OASIS, the Online Asperger Syndrome Information and Support website (www.udel.edu/bkirby/asperger) does the same for those with AD. Common sense and experience with teens with NLD or AD suggest that continued support will be needed for many years and that helping these teens prepare for the demands of adulthood will be necessary.

At Orion, our work with high school students led us to create the Pathways Program in 2004, a postsecondary program working on transitional support for our students. Our experiences with these students in general, and particularly with the Pathways Program, have shown us that some very specific skills are needed for making the transition into adulthood. These skills fall into three major areas, and each student will vary in ability among the three areas: life skills, love, and organizational skills.

**Life skills:** This includes the skills covered in social skills programs and transitional programs. See appendix E for an outline of the skills to be addressed over a four-year high school curriculum. Deficits in this area are most likely to get in the way of success in school or work and in developing close relationships as an adult. For this reason, we see focusing on life skills as key in the transitional years.

**Love:** All of us need to be loved, and the person with NLD or AD is no different in this regard. These young adults may not be the party animals of their age group, and most of them continue to find large social gatherings uncomfortable. But the need for a close friend or love interest is real and necessary. Family can provide an important buffer in this area, helping the person with NLD or AD avoid loneliness and isolation. However, it is essential that the young adult have some regular outside contact with appropriate peers. If any one issue is reported by our graduates as the most difficult to handle, it is the loss of a daily social group and the ensuing sense of loneliness. One student who graduated from Orion to attend a local community college provides a striking example of the difficulties our students encounter in young adulthood: His parents work and he lives at home, driving himself to school every day. Academically, things are going well for him, but what he notices and finds most difficult is that an entire day can go by without anyone saying hello to him. He misses the peer group he enjoyed at Orion. This student has benefited from the Pathways Program, which offers social and support gatherings for graduates twice a week. This allows him to stay connected to like-minded peers. Without access to a program like Pathways, isolation and depression could easily undermine his transition success.

**Organizational skills:** Organizational skills developed during high school are very important to success in postsecondary programs, whether they are academic or related to employment. The individual's ability to function independently, to use organizational strategies, and to advocate for herself are key elements to success. Keeping track of classes and assignments, developing effective study strategies, and using technology to support organization are all important skills that need to follow the student into adulthood.

I have seen many students who say that in college they want to be "normal" and not reveal their disability to anyone, even if that means forgoing services available to help them in college. This is a serious mistake and a setup for failure. Parents are usually tempted to support this idea, especially those who are still holding on to the hope that their child may be "cured." A word to the wise: Don't fall for it. As tempting as it may be to hide the needs of the adult with NLD or AD at school or work, the end result is an unnecessary pressure to be something she is not, living a lie that adds to depression and anxiety, and often contributes to failure in achieving her goals.

## College

Though college presents certain challenges to those with NLD or AD, it can also represent a light at the end of the tunnel—a chance to transition into an independent adult life. Most of these young adults are academically capable of attending college. The question is whether they are prepared organizationally and socially for the demands of college. Many parents we see have the mistaken idea that a community college is a better option than a four-year college for their child. In part, this is based on the realization that their child is not socially ready to live in a dorm or apartment. This idea also arises because parents see the academic demands of a two-year program as less overwhelming organizationally. This could not be further from the truth.

The organizational demands of the community college system seem to combine the worst of the comprehensive high schools with the worst of the four-year colleges. The classes are large (more than one hundred students in some cases), and there is little college-campus life that includes and supports kids with NLD or AD. Students we have worked with describe the social milieu as packs of kids roaming together, many staying connected to their high school social groups because they aren't challenged by the demands of moving to a four-year college and having to live away from home. As a group, the population is either students just out of high school or older adults coming back for a specific purpose. This is hardly a welcoming social environment for kids with NLD or AD. In general, community colleges have limited technological supports and their faculty is unprepared to meet the needs of students with NLD or AD.

Yet, in all colleges, there are supports available under IDEA. Community colleges have a department charged with identifying students who qualify for services and supporting those services; these are usually named something like Disabled Student Services (DSS) or Student Support Services. It's important to be an informed consumer. Schools will advertise these services and many tout what a great program they have, but obtaining those services can be challenging. For example, one community college with a DSS program identifies qualified students and proudly describes what they offer. One of the accommodations students with NLD or AD are entitled to is extended time for taking tests. In fact, this accommodation is generally available at any school, but the reality of getting the service is another thing. At this particular community college, the student has to be identified as qualified by DSS, and then the student (not a

DSS counselor) has to notify every instructor of the accommodation they are entitled to—extended time on tests. They must also notify the professor a week in advance of each test or quiz of their need to take the test in a separate setting to allow for extended time—every single time they have a test or quiz. Then, on the day of the test, they must go to the class, get the test from the instructor (sometimes in front of the entire class), and then proceed to find the assigned room for taking the test with a DSS proctor. Needless to say, few if any students follow though with this burdensome process.

What does seem to be successful is the support offered at small private colleges. Although the big four-year universities are prestigious and very attractive to gifted kids with NLD or AD and their parents, they are too big. The classes and campus life are overwhelming. These schools may be a great option for graduate school, but these students need undergraduate education that is more personalized and allows for contact with professors. Small private schools are also more likely to have a student services department that provides good follow-up and to have technology to support the organizational needs of students with NLD or AD. Yet even the best of the college settings to date doesn't adequately address the social needs of students with NLD or AD. This remains an area of great concern.

There may be light at the end of the tunnel. In the past few years, a number of private businesses have been established with the specific goal of providing the transitional support in life skills needed by young adults with neurocognitive disorders. They are not colleges, but are located in cities with a variety of postsecondary options (two-year and four-year colleges, technological institutes, and various job-training programs). In these programs, participants live in an apartment with a roommate, and staff members work with them on things like cooking and budgeting, laundry, and how to maintain their time schedules. They also offer evening activities, both social and educational, and counselors for coaching in life skills. These programs allow the individual to transition away from home and toward independence. Unfortunately, such programs are very expensive and, so far, not covered by insurance or government programs. Nonetheless, this is an excellent approach and worth looking into for young adults who aren't ready for dorm or apartment life but are ready to try taking a step toward independence.

One difficulty for the families of young adults with NLD or AD is knowing when they are ready for that next step. Those with NLD or AD may not be able to tell when they're ready, and given their general reluctance to change, discussion of life after high school is often difficult and painful. As a parent, it is important to be clear about what your goals are and what your beliefs are about your child's abilities. If you firmly believe your child will never be able to live on her own, then you must plan accordingly. This includes seeking professional help to establish a trust for her after you pass away and setting her up with the programs and support she may qualify for, such as Social Security Insurance (SSI), state and regional programs, and work support programs from your state Department of Social Services. However, if you believe your child has some chance for an independent life, it is very important to refrain from overprotection. She will have failures and setbacks on the road to adulthood—all children do. Sometimes you'll have to take a chance, allowing your child the privilege of failure typically extended to other young adults.

## Future Research

NLD and AD are disabilities that affect many individuals, and their families, every day. Research on both is underway and needs to continue if we are to develop effective programs and better assessment practices. Professionals who are working to define these disorders need to communicate their ideas and experiences, sharing what they know or think they know. For now, in the absence of definitive knowledge, we are left with many ideas, possibilities, and opinions. As noted at the beginning of this book, it is possible that the ideas presented here may, in the future, be proven useful. For now, they are a place to start. Future research will offer new information to help define these disorders, refine programs and interventions, and enhance our ability to help children with NLD or AD achieve their full potential.

# APPENDIX A

# Resources

Children with NLD or AD are a treasure and an asset to their families and to society. Their potential is unknown and often untapped in traditional educational settings. As we have seen throughout this book, special programming is needed to allow these children to overcome the limitations their particular disabilities present. These children will need intervention and support in their day-to-day lives, beginning with early diagnosis and program planning. This planning must include a long-range vision of how to move the child toward greater effectiveness and independence and away from helplessness and a definition of himself as a weak, incompetent person or an invalid.

Knowledge empowers people, and gaining knowledge about NLD and AD is an important first step for families, professionals who work with these children, and the children themselves. Families in particular need all the information they can get. Professionals need to receive training in handling these children and providing services for them. The children need to understand their disorder, to know it is not a mystery and that they aren't so weird—that there are many children like them who struggle with the same issues. The Harry Potter books, by J. K. Rowling, are particularly popular with these children (and other children too, of course). One of the reasons children with NLD or AD love these books is because they focus on a child who is born different and who doesn't fit in but who learns about himself and discovers the magic within him. For children with NLD or AD, this discovery process is essential, and it must be guided by knowledgeable adults.

# Internet Sites

The Internet sites listed below are full of information and resources that can be extremely useful to parents and professionals interested in NLD and AD.

For nonverbal learning disorder, the following three sites are excellent:

- www.nldontheweb.org

- www.nldline.com

- www.nlda.org (the Nonverbal Learning Disability Association; NLDA)

For Asperger's disorder and related topics, the following sites are great places to start. They offer comprehensive information and links to other sources of information:

- www.udel.edu/bkirby/asperger (Online Asperger Syndrome Information and Support; OASIS)

- www.aspergersresource.org

- www.info.med.yale.edu/chldstdy/autism/index.html (Yale Developmental Disabilities Clinic)

- www.aspennj.org (Asperger Syndrome Educational Network; ASPEN)

- www.asperger.org (MAAP Services for Autism and Asperger Syndrome)

# Programs

The list below is hardly comprehensive. Be sure to consult the Internet sites listed above for information on other programs that address the needs of students with NLD or AD. However, be advised that as the diagnoses of NLD and Asperger's are becoming more known, some programs may try to advertise themselves as appropriate to these students without really having the knowledge or experience to provide quality programs. Be an informed consumer.

- **Orion Academy** (Moraga, CA; www.orionacademy.org). Grades 9 through 12. Orion was the first high school in the country designed specifically for students with NLD or Asperger's. Established in 2000, it continues to expand and is focused on developing a model program for the education of students with neurocognitive disorders. Accredited by the Western Association of Schools and Colleges, Orion offers college preparatory education for bright students. Orion also offers a postsecondary program, the Pathways Program, that provides support and social activities for young adults transitioning into local colleges or employment.

- **Bridges Academy** (Sherman Oaks, CA; www.bridges .edu). Grades 6 through 12. This school is dedicated to educating gifted students with special learning needs.

- **Raskob Institute and Day School** (Oakland, CA; www .raskobinstitute.org). Grades 2 through 8. Designed for students with language-based learning disabilities, this school has experience with kids with NLD or Asperger's. They offer small classes without the distraction of kids with behavior problems, as well as strong social support and speech and language services. Children with reading problems do very well here.

- **Star Academy** (San Anselmo, CA; www.staracademy. org). Grades 2 through 9. This day program for students with AS and high-functioning autism addresses behavior issues and provides individualized programming with less academic pressure.

- **Franklin Academy** (East Haddam, CT; www.fa-ct.org). Grades 8 through 12. This boarding and day school focuses on students with NLD and related disorders.

- **Pathways Academy** (at McLean Hospital, Boston, MA; www.mclean.harvard.edu/patient/child/cnis.php). Ages 5 to 11. This day treatment program and school has a specific focus on Asperger's, high-functioning autism, and NLD.

- **The Help Group's school** (Los Angeles, CA; www .thehelpgroup.org). This organization offers a variety of services for children with different disorders at different campuses.

- **College Internship Program** (CIP; www.collegeintern shipprogram.com). With programs in Massachusetts, Florida, and Indiana, this organization helps college students with NLD or AS develop and achieve their career potential.

- **College Living Experience** (CLE; www.cleinc.net). With programs in Colorado, Texas, and Florida, this organization assists students with special needs in completing college and transitioning into an independent adult life.

# Other Potential Resources for Parents

As mentioned several times in the book, it's a good idea for parents to put together a team of well-informed professionals experienced with NLD or AD to help the child. These professionals can help ensure programming is appropriate to the child's needs. They can also provide an invaluable lifelong support network for the child. And don't overlook the benefit that children are often willing to do things for other adults that they won't do for their parents. Local school districts or professionals who work with students with NLD or AD may have a list of referrals.

It is always important to check the references of any professional you're considering working with, making sure the person has the appropriate licenses and training as well as experience with the issues relevant to your child. Reputable professionals should be more than willing to provide information on their training, experience, and license. Although confidentiality may prevent these professionals from giving out names of other clients, it should be possible for them to supply references from other professionals in the community, for example, doctors, teachers, or other therapists.

- **Coaches:** Seek licensed professionals certified as coaches with experience in life issues and organizational skills.

- **Tutors:** Tutors can be most useful in helping students be more successful with homework. They may work in specific subjects, such as math or writing, or they may help the child with organization in general. Some are credentialed teachers who specialize in learning disabilities; others are just high school or college students or interested adults in the community. Tutors without specific training as teachers can be helpful, but parents must understand the limitations of their abilities. If program planning and working with the school is involved, it is probably a better choice to find a credentialed teacher or an educational therapist.

- **Educational therapists:** These are certified professionals with hours of specialized training. They can be very valuable in program development and in individual work with the child. They can reinforce what is being taught at school, act as a case manager for the child, and oversee the child's workload, helping parents who are not educational professionals understand the needs of their child.

- **Advocates:** These are people who specialize in special education law and work with families to develop appropriate individual education plans (IEPs). In some states, both attorneys and nonattorneys fill this role.

- **Occupational therapists:** These professionals are essential members of any team planning a program for a child with NLD or AD. An assessment by a qualified occupational therapist is a must for all such children.

- **Speech therapists:** A program plan for a child with NLD or AD that does not include at least an assessment by a qualified speech therapist will be missing a key ingredient. Speech therapists are often the professionals most directly involved in working on pragmatic language development in these children.

# APPENDIX B

# Classroom Wish List

The list below presents the contents and environment of the ideal elementary school classroom for students with NLD or AD, in no particular order:

- A gifted teacher with an open mind and a sense of humor, willing to learn about students with NLD and AD

- A student-to-teacher ratio of no more than twelve to one, at least during core academic subjects

- A classroom that promotes kindness and tolerance of differences but where problems in social interactions are dealt with as soon as they arise

- A classroom that is neat and clean and uncluttered, both physically (not too much furniture crammed into a small room) and visually (bulletin boards, whiteboards, and other teaching areas provide information simply and clearly)

- Classroom schedules that are posted and are consistent and routines that don't change without advance notice

- A teacher who follows the schedule and routine and who is very organized and predictable

- Rules that are clear and consistent and consequences that are predictable

- The availability of headphones to listen to music as needed

- Permission to get water or go to the bathroom as needed

- A second set of books at home to reduce the need to remember what needs to travel between school and home

- The availability of technology to reduce the need for handwriting, to make it easier to remember assignments, and to facilitate transfer of homework between home and school (using e-mail or networked classroom systems)

- Internet access to class assignments and to the teacher

- Class work that uses auditory cues as often as visual cues

- Worksheets that are not visually overwhelming

- Models of the finished product of assignments provided for students to review before they do their assignment

- Explicit beginning and end points of assignments, including help in keeping on track with reading and lectures in class

- Teaching that explains and reviews the main idea

- Homework that is not redundant

- Projects that teach the process of learning, not just the concepts, and that allow the child to learn about areas of personal interest

- A curriculum that includes social skills training as part of the overall teaching plan, not just as an adjunct program offered once or twice a week

- Recess that has adequate adult supervision and access to supervised activities and noncompetitive games

- Technology that is integrated into the overall program, not tacked on as an afterthought and not understood by the staff

- A teacher who is excited by the use of technology in the classroom

- Access to a challenging curriculum

- Regular consultation for teachers and staff to review students' specific needs in terms of curriculum and behavioral issues (which would actually be great for all students)

# APPENDIX C

# Activities for Children with NLD or AD

Unlike most of their age-mates, children and teens with NLD or AD often find themselves with few outside activities. In many cases, parents find that social differences limit their child's success in activities outside the home. However, this need not be the case, and the sooner the child is exposed to outside activities, the better. This is not to say that any given program is going to work. Careful selection is necessary. This includes limiting the size of the group, sensory stimulation, competition, and other such demands. But with the right activity, the child may reap significant benefits. Beyond having fun and gaining experience in social interaction, the child may develop skills and strengths that will be useful later in life. Here are some activities that have been successful for kids with NLD or AD.

**Martial arts:** Various schools of martial arts teach self-discipline and individual success, not group success. For kids with NLD or AD, being a part of a group is hard enough; having to perform as part of that group (as in team sports) is harder to understand and accomplish. In martial arts, the rules are consistent and the practice is a good way to build strength.

**Swimming:** Swimming is often a team sport, but the swimmers are usually only competing against their own previous times. Being in water provides some children with NLD or AD a measure of relief from their sense of clumsiness. A note of caution: For some of these children, the feel of being in the water is one of the sensory experiences they find disturbing. Early exposure and frequent access helps limit this difficulty. Never force a child into the water; the anxiety that results can obliterate any benefits that would be gained. Encouragement and making a game of playing in water will be more likely to create the positive atmosphere that can develop into an interest in swimming.

**Girl Scouts (and potentially Boy Scouts):**  As a group, Girl Scouts is supportive of differences, teaches cooperation, and offers many wonderful experiences in a supervised group setting. Choose the troop carefully. Look for a small troop with experienced and understanding leaders. It may be necessary for parents to participate in the activities, at least in the younger grades, as an "out" for the child with NLD or AD if the social situation becomes overwhelming. Boy Scouts has the potential to offer the same advantages as Girl Scouts; it depends on the leader's ability to accept differences and make accommodations. The positives to be gained are many, and the experiences can help the child with NLD or Asperger's develop flexibility.

**4-H clubs and other clubs:**  Look for groups that allow for both group and individual projects and are organized around a topic or activity of interest to the child. Many children with NLD or Asperger's have a great affinity for animals, and this is often a wonderful avenue for outside activities. Others prefer music, history, chess, or role-playing games. If you are a parent, become involved in your child's interests. If you work at a school, try to offer opportunities for children with NLD or Asperger's to participate in activities with others and fit in.

**Bowling:**  For whatever reason, this seems to be an activity that many children with NLD or Asperger's enjoy, even though it's visual-spatial in nature. "Bumper bowling," where the gutter is filled with a bumper, is clearly preferable, but as the child gets older this may be embarrassing.

**Library activities and volunteer opportunities:** In many communities, public libraries offer a wealth of activities for elementary-age children that are pleasurable and quiet and that expose the child to information in an enjoyable venue. The child's interest in information can develop into a volunteer or work opportunity for older children and teens.

**Local animal or wildlife organizations:** Animals often provide a nonjudgmental relationship for these children. Many breeds of dog, in particular, are forgiving of human social mistakes and happy to get attention from people who love them. In many areas, local animal rescue groups or wildlife rescue organizations have interesting activities, classes, and training opportunities. The training may lead to a job as a helper, or in some cases for the teen who is ready for this, a docent job.

# APPENDIX D

# Information Processing Deficits

Information processing deficits affect the three key areas of dysfunction in nonverbal learning disorder and Asperger's disorder. The information presented here is based on work with NLD children. It is likely that AD children are affected in a similar way, although not all aspects of these deficits affect all children in the same way. The problems that result from deficits in information processing appear to be interconnected, and the combination creates the disorder that is NLD.

## Deficits in Organizational Skills and Executive Function

### Organization

- Difficulties with novel situations and learning

- Slow processing speed

- Rigid thinking

- Concrete interpretation

- Perfectionism

- Focus on the wrong details

- Difficulty with "if-then" thinking

## Integration

- Poor tolerance of frustration; gives up easily

- Limited production of work production; feels overwhelmed by a heavy load

- Difficulty creating written documents

- Rigid and perfectionistic about work

- Easily overwhelmed; often shuts down emotionally

## Production

- Fails to comprehend the main idea

- May see all details as equally important

- Has poor ability to understand and use metaphor and analogy

- Has difficulty reading between the lines

- Relies on pattern learning and misses key concepts

- Prefers a step-by-step, sequential mode of learning, and often loses sight of the whole concept in the process

# Visual-Spatial and Sensory-Motor Integration Deficits

- Is clumsy

- May not explore the world through physical activity; uses language instead

- Processes visual information slowly or ineffectively

- Has poor hand-to-eye coordination

- Has facial recognition problems; affects ability to read social situations

- Often exhibits poor eye contact

- Has body posture problems and limp, weak muscle tone

- Has difficulty producing handwriting

- Confused about directions and may get lost easily

- Has difficulty maintaining attention

- Unsure of own body boundaries

- Sensitive to tactile, auditory, and visual stimuli

## Social Skills Deficits

- Difficulty writing for and interacting with the "audience"

- Difficulty taking the perspective of another person

- Difficulty conceptualizing what they are talking about; losing sight of the audience's interest or comprehension

- Poor entry into and exit from conversation

- Poor or sporadic grooming

- Cognitive and behavioral rigidity

- Poor integration of multiple levels of information, which is required in social settings

- Difficulty predicting outcomes, which makes all interactions novel

- Difficulty managing anxiety

- Failure to think about how other people feel

- Problems with time and time references

- Trouble with novel situations

- Limited range of feelings

- Difficulty with give-and-take in social situations

- Poor ability to understand nuances

# Orion Academy's Social Skills and Transitional Program: Outline and Goals

Orion Academy is dedicated not just to the academic success of students with NLD or AD, but also to their success in life. To this end, we've developed a comprehensive program in life skills. After establishing a solid foundation of social skills in the freshman and sophomore years, we build on those skills in junior and senior year and also add skills for transitioning into an independent life as an adult, whether that be at college or work.

## Freshman Year

### Basic Social Skills

- Eye contact
    - Using eye contact when talking to others to acknowledge that one is listening
- Body language
    - Using body language to indicate that one is listening

- An ability to read subtle body language clues and report on those cues

- Conversational skills

  - Taking turns in conversation, not interrupting others, and allowing others to join conversation

  - Flexibility in regard to topic and an ability to continue flow when the topic changes

  - Entering and exiting a conversation without help

- Emotions

  - Identifying one's own emotions when asked

  - Reading others' facial expressions when asked

  - Appropriately expressing one's own emotions

- Peer relationships

  - Introducing oneself appropriately

  - Friendship management: asking for and accepting feedback on skills; developing and maintaining at least one friendship

  - Using the phone

  - Making plans for after school at least once a session

- Self-care skills

  - Basic hygiene: showering, shaving, wearing clean clothes, avoiding bad breath, and so on

  - Sleep management

  - Taking medication, with reminders

  - Understanding healthy nutrition

- Psychoeducation
  - Learning about nonverbal learning disorder and Asperger's disorder
  - Understanding why social skills are important

### Field Trip Goals

- Developing basic transportation skills (for example, taking public transportation or reading a map)
- Socializing in a group setting with patience and willingness to compromise

### Expectations from Home

- Practicing transportation skills
- Supporting friendship management skills
- Supporting self-care skills at home

Additionally, freshmen participate in a level I Alert Program, taught jointly by an occupational therapist and a psychologist. In this program, they learn various self-regulation strategies, and teachers reinforce and encourage students to use their chosen Alert strategies. Alert Program tools, such as candies, squishy balls, and T-stools, are available in all classrooms.

# Sophomore Year

## Social Skills

- Manners
  - Appropriate eating behaviors and cleaning up after oneself
  - Pleasantries (hello, good-bye, and the like)

- Requesting help and handling confrontations
- Developing a sense of body boundaries

- Peer relationships
  - Understanding teasing and avoiding engaging in it
  - Maintaining and expanding friendships to more than one person: organizing get-togethers; creating a friendship group

- Time management
  - Planning ahead
  - Using a watch
  - Taking responsibility for time management

- Organizational skills
  - Taking responsibility for class work and maintaining grades
  - Using reminder strategies taught at school

- Stress and anxiety management
  - Understanding stress and anxiety
  - Learning strategies to reduce stress and anxiety

## Psychoeducation

- Understanding one's medication and taking it without reminders

## Field Trip Goals

- Advanced transportation skills (for example, reading a map)

- Socializing in a group setting

- Time management

- Organizational skills (such as planning the trip)

### Expectations from Home

- Encouraging the student to get together with peers outside of Orion once a month

- Encouraging use of time management skills (using an alarm, arriving at school on time, and so on)

- Supporting the student in taking responsibility for medications at home

Additionally, sophomores participate in a level II Alert Program where they learn about stress, effects of stress, and various strategies to relieve stress and anxiety, such as meditation, visualization, exercise, sleep, and nutrition.

# Junior Year

### Social Skills

- Empathy

  - Learning to read nonverbal cues or feelings in others and respond accordingly

  - Learning how to convey an understanding of others' feelings

- Assertiveness skills and conflict resolution

  - Giving and receiving criticism and compliments

  - Handling peer pressure

  - Advocating for oneself appropriately, especially in the school setting

## Transitional Skills

- Responsibility and independence skills

    - Arriving on time to school, classes, events

    - Completing work on time (less reliance on home-work club)

    - Notifying others when absent or late

    - Scheduling doctors appointments

    - Doing chores at home to overlap with living skills

    - Living skills, including cleaning one's room and maintaining clothing

- Job skills

    - Learning how to search for jobs

    - Developing a resume

    - Practicing interview skills

- College planning

    - Learning how to search for colleges

    - Visiting a college campus

    - Completing a Personal Project on searching for jobs or colleges

    - Participating in a volunteer or internship program (optional but recommended)

- Legal rights and accessing resources

    - Understanding the Individuals with Disabilities Act (IDEA)

    - Determining what services one will need in college or a job and how to get them

## Psychoeducation

- Understanding psychological issues one may encounter

    - Depression

    - Anxiety

    - How NLD or Asperger's can affect one's college or job experience

    - Identifying helpful resources for dealing with these issues

## Field Trip Goals

- Planning transportation for more complex travel, including trips with multiple destinations or transfer points

- Developing an ability to interact with members of the community

- Exploring resources for life after Orion

## Expectations from Home

- Regular performance of independence skills (doing laundry, grocery shopping, keeping up with appointments, preparing lunch, driving or using public transportation, and so on)

- Exploring possibilities for life after Orion (for example, visiting a college or finding a local job)

# Senior Year

## Transitional Skills

- Job searching

- Using the Internet

- Filling out applications

- Developing interview skills and participating in mock interviews

- College searching

  - Being aware of what questions are important to ask when researching colleges

  - Meeting deadlines and getting necessary information

- Independence skills

  - Planning and scheduling activities

  - Solving problems

  - Setting goals

  - Employment skills and interview skills

  - Preparing for emergencies

- Young adult issues

  - Dating

  - Identity issues

  - Turning eighteen and legal rights

- Preparation for graduation

  - Meeting requirements

  - Graduation speeches

### Field Trip Goals

- Senior field trips address all social skills addressed in social skills group at Orion Academy and include the Senior Challenge (described below), which is required for graduation.

### Expectations from Home

- Encouraging money management, such as managing one's allowance and spending it on wanted items

- Supporting and adding to the independence skills of all four years

- Supporting the community service requirement, including completion of all paperwork and documentation

At the end of their senior year, all students participate in the Senior Challenge, a scavenger hunt in which students solve clues and complete a number of tasks, such as interacting with members of the community, navigating around town, using maps, asking directions, ordering food, and managing money. Students stay overnight at a hotel in a nearby city.

# References

American Psychiatric Association (APA). 1994. *Diagnostic and Statistical Manual of Mental Disorders.* 4th edition. Washington, DC: American Psychiatric Association.

Asperger, H. 1944. Autistic psychopathy in childhood. Translated by U. Frith. In *Autism and Asperger's Syndrome,* ed. U. Frith, 37-92. Cambridge: Cambridge University Press.

Attwood, T. 1997. *Asperger's Syndrome: A Guide for Parents and Professionals.* London: Jessica Kingsley Publications.

Autism and Developmental Disorders Monitoring Network. 2007. *Prevalence of the Autism Spectrum Disorders (ASDs) in Multiple Areas of the United States, 2000 and 2002.* Washington, DC: Centers for Disease Control, 2007.

Baron-Cohen, S. 1995. *Mindblindness: An Essay on Autism and Theory of Mind.* Cambridge, MA: MIT Press.

Cumine, V., J. Leach, and G. Stevenson. 1998. *Asperger Syndrome: A Practical Guide for Teachers.* London: David Fulton Publishers.

Dawson, G., C. Finley, S. Phillips, and L. Galpert. 1986. Hemispheric specialization and the language abilities of autistic children. *Child Development* 57(6):1440-1453.

Duke, M. P., S. Nowicki, and E. A. Martin. 1996. *Teaching Your Child the Language of Social Success.* Atlanta: Peachtree.

Ehlers, S., and C. Gillberg. 1993. The epidemiology of Asperger's syndrome: A total population study. *Journal of Child Psychology and Psychiatry, and Allied Disciplines*, 34(8):1327-1350.

Gray, C. 1994. *Comic Strip Conversations*. Arlington, TX: Future Horizons.

Hilts, P. L. 2001. Panel finds earlier autism tests will lead to better treatment. *New York Times*, June 15, A16.

Hsu, L. 2001. The books. In *Sacred Grounds Anthology #6* 3(2). Oakland, CA: Minotaur Press.

Humphries, N. 1992. *A History of the Mind: Evolution and the Birth of Consciousness*. New York: Simon & Schuster.

Johnson, D., and H. Myklebust. 1971. *Learning Disabilities*. New York: Grune & Stratton.

Klin, A., F. R. Volkmar, S. S. Sparrow, D. V. Cicchetti, and B. P. Rourke. 1995. Validity and neuropsychological characterization of Asperger's syndrome: Convergence with nonverbal learning disabilities syndrome. *Journal of Child Psychology and Psychiatry, and Allied Disciplines* 36(7):1127-1140.

Kralovec, E., and J. Buell. *The End of Homework: How Homework Disrupts Families, Overburdens Children, and Limits Learning*. Boston: Beacon Press, 2000.

March, J. S., and K. Mulle. 1998. *OCD in Children and Adolescents: A Cognitive-Behavioral. Treatment Manual*. New York: Guilford Press.

McGee, R., M. Feehan, S. Williams, E. Partridge, P. Silva, and J. Kelle. 1990. DSM III disorders in a large sample of adolescents. *Journal of the American Academy of Child and Adolescent Psychiatry* 29(4):611-619.

Merikangas, K., S. Avenevoli, L. Dierker, and C. Grillon. 1999. Vulnerability factors among children at risk for anxiety disorders. *Biological Psychiatry* 46(11):1523-1535.

Myklebust, H. R. 1975. Nonverbal learning disabilities: Assessment and intervention. In *Progress in Learning Disabilities*, ed. H. R. Myklebust, vol. 3, 85-121. New York: Grune & Stratton.

National Institute of Neurological Disorders and Stroke. 2007. Asperger's syndrome fact sheet. Available at www.ninds.nih.gov/disorders/asperger/detail_asperger.htm.

Nowicki, S., and M. P. Duke. 1992. *Helping the Child Who Doesn't Fit In*. Atlanta: Peachtree.

Puce, A., T. Allison, S. Bentin, J. C. Gore, and G. McCarthy. 1998. Temporal cortex activation in humans viewing eye and mouth movements. *Journal of Neuroscience* 18(6):2188-2199.

Raine, A., T. E. Moffitt, A. Caspi, R. Loeber, M. Stouthamer-Loeber, and D. Lynam. 2005. Neurocognitive impairments in boys on the life-course persistent antisocial path. *Journal of Abnormal Psychology* 114(1):38-49.

Rourke, B. 1989. *Nonverbal Learning Disability: The Syndrome and the Model*. New York: Guilford Press.

———. 1995. *Syndrome of Nonverbal Learning Disability: Neuro-developmental Manifestations*. New York: Guilford Press.

———. 1998. *Syndrome of Nonverbal Learning Disability: Assessment Protocol*. nldontheweb.org.

Schultz, R. T., I. Gauthier, R. Fulbright, A. W. Anderson, C. Lacadie, P. Skudlarski, M. J. Tarr, D. J. Cohen, and J. C. Gore. 1997. Are face identity and emotion processed automatically? Abstracts of the Third International Conference on Functional Mapping of the Human Brain, Copenhagen, Denmark, May 17-22, 1997. *Neuroimage* 5(suppl 4):S148.

Thompson, S. 1996. *The Source for Nonverbal Learning Disorders*. East Moline, IL: LinguiSystems.

U.S. Department of Education. 1999. *Twenty-First Annual Report to Congress on the Implementation of the Individuals with*

*Disabilities Education Act.* Washington, DC: U.S. Department of Education.

Vasa, R. A., and D. S. Pine. 2004. Neurobiology. In *Anxiety Disorders in Children and Adolescents,* 2nd edition, eds. T. L. Morris and J. S. March, 3-26. New York: Guilford Press.

Vatterott, C., 2003. There's something wrong with homework. *Principal* 82(3):64.

Volkmar, F., and A. Klin. 1998. Asperger's syndrome and nonverbal learning disabilities. In *Asperger's Syndrome or High-Functioning Autism?* eds. E. Schopler, G. Mesibov, and L. Kunec, 107-122. New York: Plenum Press.

Volkmar, F. R., A. Klin, R. T. Schultz, E. Rubin, and R. Bronen. 2000. Asperger's disorder. *American Journal of Psychiatry* 157(2):262-267.

Williams, M., and A. Shellenberger. 1994. *How Does Your Engine Run? A Leader's Guide to the Alert Program for Sensory Regulation.* Albuquerque, NM: TherapyWorks.

Wing, L. 1981. Asperger's syndrome: A clinical account. *Psychological Medicine* 11(1):115-130.

**Kathryn Stewart, Ph.D.,** is a clinical psychologist specializing in child, adolescent, and family therapy, and a leading expert in treating neurocognitve disorders in children. She is the founder and executive director of the Orion Academy, in Moraga, CA, the first college-preparatory high school for students with NLD and Asperger's disorder. She is a leading expert and frequent speaker on the topic of NLD and Asberger's for various psychological associations, such as the LDA.

# more titles for **smart, effective parenting**
## from new**harbinger**publications

**HELPING YOUR CHILD WITH SELECTIVE MUTISM**

$14.95 • Item Code: 416X

**TEACH ME HOW TO SAY IT RIGHT**

$14.95 • Item Code: 4038

**HELPING YOUR CHILD WITH AUTISM SPECTRUM DISORDER**

$17.95 • Item Code: 3848

**KID COOPERATION**

$15.95 • Item Code: 0407

**THE BALANCED MOM**

$14.95 • Item Code: 4534